Gayle Peterson · Robert Yawson · Ellen J. K. · Jeremy Nicholls

Navigating Big Finance and Big Technology for Global Change

The Impact of Social Finance on the World's Poor

palgrave
macmillan

Gayle Peterson
Said Business School
University of Oxford
Oxford, UK

Ellen J. K.
Anon, UK

Robert Yawson
Quinnipiac University
Hamden, CT, USA

Jeremy Nicholls
Social Value International
Liverpool, UK

ISSN 2662-5105 ISSN 2662-5113 (electronic)
Palgrave Studies in Impact Finance
ISBN 978-3-030-40714-8 ISBN 978-3-030-40712-4 (eBook)
https://doi.org/10.1007/978-3-030-40712-4

Cover credit: Gavin Douglas/Concern Worldwide

This Palgrave Macmillan imprint is published by the registered company Springer Nature Switzerland AG
The registered company address is: Gewerbestrasse 11, 6330 Cham, Switzerland

Preface

This book was written to help new social investors do good, avoid harm, and never have to resort to the refrain, "If only we'd known." It pays particular attention to the potential of money and technology to improve the current and future lives of vulnerable people, and aid the regeneration of our fragile planet. It also provides warning signs of common perils—the things that can go wrong and how to avoid them. Through case illustrations, the authors discuss ways to measure and be held accountable for positive and negative impacts. They provide examples of successful approaches used by colleagues in finance and technology sectors to address the world's Wicked Problems and, in some cases, make money doing so. Finally, we hope our analysis helps navigate the ethical decisions investors face when balancing purpose and profit. In the end, while we can't help everyone avoid all the pitfalls, we hope it will make the path a lot clearer.

Big business needs to do good with its profits. Big Technology needs to stop doing harm. And we all need to act "bigger" quickly because, according to the experts, we don't have much time.

The 17 United Nations (UN) Sustainable Development Goals (SDGs) exemplify the daunting real-life challenges facing humanity and the planet—climate change, inequality and poverty, and destruction of our oceans, forests, and biodiversity, among other things. Are they complete? Probably not: despite providing a lengthy inventory of the elements sustainable development involves, there are other landmine issues not included in the SDGs. For example, they do not capture threats to sustainable development such as the weakening of democracy aided by "big technology," and do not grasp the devastating implications of the Fourth Industrial Revolution on the global workforce. They present a picture of what the world should be like, rather than scenarios of what it might be like depending on what actions are taken or ignored.

Nonetheless, they provide a road map for saving the planet at a time when, given the urgency of action, an accurate map or a strong GPS signal is very much needed. That the SDG map shows us are the landmarks on the sustainable development journey, and where the rest stops and repair shops are. What the map doesn't tell us is who else is on the road, which direction they are travelling in, and at what speed. A map is helpful, but it doesn't by itself prevent accidents and disasters. In addition to accurate maps, a safe road journey needs elements like a highway code that is understood and adhered to by all drivers, standards of vehicle safety so that drivers have reliable accelerators and brakes, and a well-maintained environment so that we have good visibility and are spared dangerous corners or hazardous road surfaces. In short, a safe, successful journey is not simply about understanding the destination; it is dependent on multiple interconnected elements, many of which are beyond our control.

The importance of something more than a map—something more like an understanding of interconnected systems—came to the fore in 2020 with the arrival of the COVID-19 pandemic. The rapid effect of the virus on global social and economic life highlighted how messy and interconnected the world has become. The virus spread from country to country, brutally disrupting industries and social norms. Rapidly and brutally, it held economic and sociopolitical systems up to the harshest of lights. It exposed their frailties, false assumptions, and contradictions as countries tried to find an appropriate response; but it also showed how things that a few months earlier would have been considered "impossible" were not only possible but desirable once the magnitude of the problem had been understood. Be it lockdowns, government social welfare expenditures, investment in public health, or any number of other interventions affecting people's individual and collective lives, it was not just possible but essential that we turn the unimaginable into the norm.

The lessons from the COVID-19 pandemic are only starting to be learned, but there are already insights emerging that are relevant to the themes of this book:

Insight 1: What may seem like local problems, quickly escalate into ones that are global, spread by the global interconnectedness that is taken for granted as the norm.

Insight 2: As the "problem" spreads, it becomes apparent that it cannot be "solved" in the way a puzzle can. It is not something that stands alone; it is part of a mess of tightly interwoven issues that feed into each other, generating new problems that require a fundamental rethinking of what is necessary and possible.

Insight 3: What seemed a short while ago "impossible," becomes possible in a short space of time. Moreover, things we took for granted as normal, are quickly overturned. There are many examples of this including false assumptions that national wealth always equates with better health outcomes—the reality is that "rich" USA and Britain suffered far more than "poor" Indonesia and the Philippines. But as important for this book is how quickly "the normal" changed. Long-held views about social welfare safety nets, public health, and the use of government funds were discarded in quick time, replaced by policies and programs that were previously thought beyond the pale.

Each of these insights has relevance beyond COVID-19. They are important for understanding the complex, messy, interrelated issues that make up the most pressing challenges of our time. Those challenges—things like climate change, inclusion, poverty, threats to life on land and underwater—come together to form "Wicked Problems," the kind of problem mentioned earlier is not to be seen as a puzzle to be solved. Wicked Problems are messy, chaotic, and threaten what we might consider the "norm." But if they cannot be solved, they can be remedied or tamed. To do this, however, takes a certain kind of leadership which we call "Deliberate Leadership," characterized among other things as courageous, collaborative, and creative. The central argument of this book is that Big Finance and Big Technology are so large and far-reaching in the modern world that they are inevitably an element in any Wicked Problem. At the very least, they need to ensure they do not exacerbate the situation; but more than that, they need to exhibit the Deliberate Leadership that will increase their contribution to sustainable development in ways that befit their size and influence. One of the ways they can contribute is through Social Finance which, at the risk of over-simplification, refers to the allocation of capital primarily for social and environmental returns, or the remedy of complex social/environmental challenges.

Can this book save the planet from wickedly difficult problems? Probably not. But it can be a helpful primer for those using money and technology to achieve the SDGs, while avoiding common pitfalls that can harm the vulnerable people and planet they seek to serve. We recognize how money and technology can work to degenerate rather than regenerate society and the environment, but we also share examples of what works when Big Finance and Big Technology step in to solve big problems, not least through social finance. In doing so, we hope positive impact can be accelerated and deliberate leadership become more widespread. This book draws on our research and empirical case studies resulting from interviews with more than 1500 interviews with social investors in more than 20 countries. These conversations with CEOs working in social investing (philanthropy, impact investing, public funding, intermediary support) in the BRIC (Brazil, Russia, India, and China) to countries in Africa, Europe, and North America. We gathered frank, discerning, and inspiring insights into what works and what doesn't when using social finance to solve Wicked Problems.

Written as an anthology, this book offers perspectives from seasoned (and often bruised from trying) academics, advocates, and advisors. We share both successes and cautionary tales about harm that can occur through uninformed, and often unchecked, social investments, whether philanthropy, impact investing, or traditional finance.

Advisor and academics Gayle Peterson and Robert Yawson guide readers through an introduction to common definitions, social finance and SDGs, and provide a Deliberate Leadership framework to help investors find their North Star to make more ethical decisions when confronting wickedly difficult problems. Tom Van Dyck, managing director and financial advisor of Royal Bank of Canada (RBC), shares his path for making money with mission by embedding a Divest Invest approach into ESG (environmental, social, governance) investment portfolios. ESG challenges are further brought to life through the experiences of the McKnight Foundation developing a Carbon Efficiency Strategy with colleagues at BNY Mellon Capital. Jeremy Nicholls, Social Value founder and self-proclaimed grumpy consultant, challenges readers and the field to consider adopting social accounting practices to track and measure impact. The authors also write about ways technology can both accelerate positive social change and undercut advancements. The final chapter ends with stories of positive prototypes and what can be achieved when committed people use capital and technology for good. We draw on case studies of UBS Optimus Foundation's Educate Girls Development Impact Bond and the Future-Fit Foundation which is working to bring companies from all sectors to tackle Wicked Problems more purposefully, and at the same time enable investors to use their position to accelerate change.

These are the toughest of times when we must face the severe consequences of our inaction on climate, slavery, poverty, and injustice, but as *Guardian* contributor and writer Richard Flanagan has said, "*We will discover the language of hope in the quality of our courage*" (Flanagan 2019). The book shares wisdom from courageous people who are using social finance to take risks, experiment, struggle, learn, and adapt their strategies to become more successful when tackling the world's difficult problems. And that should give us all hope.

Oxford, UK — Gayle Peterson
Hamden, USA — Robert Yawson
Anon, UK — Ellen J. K.
Liverpool, UK — Jeremy Nicholls

Reference

Flanagan, Richard. 2019. "Six Sentences of Hope: Defining a Unifying Vision in the Face of the Climate Crisis." *The Guardian*, August 21, 2019. https://www.theguardian.com/environment/2019/aug/22/six-sentences-of-hope-defining-a-unifying-vision-in-the-face-of-the-climate-crisis.

Acknowledgments

Special thanks to Thomas Van Dyck, managing director at SRI Wealth Management, RBC Wealth Management, for contributing significant content for Chapter 3 which explores the role of Big Finance in achieving social change. Tom has been a supporter of investments that meet environmental, social, and governance (ESG) criteria for 35 years—long before they became fashionable in the financial community. He founded As You Show, a shareholder campaign group. He has an estimated $2.6bn of client assets placed in mutual funds, ETFs, hedge funds and private equity that have been screened by ESG criteria. Tom is driven to ensure client investments align with their values.

Thanks to Dr. Michael Blowfield as developmental editor, and John Sherman, co-founder of pfc social impact advisors, for his research and contributions to summarizing case content.

We also appreciate the support of Partners for a New Economy (P4NE) and their efforts to create financial and economic systems that support an equitable and sustainable world.

Contents

List of Figures

List of Tables

CHAPTER 1

Big Finance, Big Technology, Wicked Problems, and the World's Poor

The Basics: What Are Big Finance, Big Tech, Social Finance, and Wicked Problems?

Let's begin at the beginning with some common language and concepts. What do we mean when we say Big Finance, Big Tech, social finance, and Wicked Problems? First, let's follow the money—who makes it, manages it, and who is doing good with it?

For a start, globally, the International Finance Corporation (IFC)—a member of the World Bank group—estimates there is as much as $269 trillion in financial assets held by institutions and households (IFC 2019). These assets are managed by banks, pension funds, Development Finance Institutions (DFI), private investment firms, foundations, and family offices—we collectively refer to these institutions as Big Finance. (Money hidden in a mattress doesn't count.) In addition to the traditional financial returns, Big Finance is also using capital to achieve social and environmental returns, and the commitment is growing thanks in large part to client pressure by Generation Z, millennials, and women. This is a potentially transformative period in finance aligning interest of clients, the needs of private investors, and the call for funding of the UN Sustainable Development Goals. IFC, the world's largest DFI, estimates that "investor appetite for impact investing is as high as $26 trillion—$21 trillion in publicly traded stocks and bonds, and $5 trillion in private markets involving private equity, non-sovereign private debt, and venture

G. Peterson et al., *Navigating Big Finance and Big Technology for Global Change*, Palgrave Studies in Impact Finance,
https://doi.org/10.1007/978-3-030-40712-4_1

capital …. Private impact funds currently total around \$71 billion. Larger amounts are invested by DFIs, including more than \$700 billion by those following harmonized measurement metrics, and in green and social bonds (over \$400 billion outstanding). In addition, a share of the \$8 trillion dedicated to activist investing in public markets may be managed for impact …. Green bonds have grown from around \$10 billion in 2013 to \$183 billion in 2018" (IFC 2019).

With the growth in the demand for new green and socially responsible investments comes the growth in "greenwashing" and the potential for deceptive claims (*Financial Times* 2019). There are efforts to develop principles for stopping "impact washing." For example, the IFC developed Operating Principles for Impact Management to avoid problems in the field (IFC 2019). These principles are being adopted by watchdog advocacy organization, Accountability Counsel, calling out negative impacts in the international development and impact investing space. It has encouraged IFC to expand its principles and give greater community voice and oversight throughout the life of an investment to ensure safeguards for vulnerable communities. There is a growing call for greater scrutiny and more principled money with the rapid growth of the social finance market principles and the drive to leverage the trillions needed in private capital to achieve the SDGs with integrity.

What About Big Tech?

Forbes' 2019 'Global 2000' ranking of public companies calls out the largest and most successful companies on the planet, and tech businesses "account for more than \$9 trillion in market value, \$4 trillion in assets, and nearly \$3 trillion in sales" (Ponciano 2019). In 2000, tech companies continued to grow in value, making up 10% of the top 100 firms. The five biggest tech companies in the world—Amazon, Apple, Facebook, Microsoft, and Google's parent company Alphabet are collectively worth hundreds of billions of dollars, exceeding the value of economies of countries as big as Saudi Arabia. As well as these United States-headquartered brands, there are Asian companies such as Tencent and Alibaba that are part of the powerful Big Tech mix.

Big Tech companies drive Big Finance. Apple continues to be in first place as the most successful tech company in the world with an estimated \$267 billion in revenue in 2019. In the end, this massive amount of money is managed somewhere in the world by big financial institutions.

There are dark and light, negative and positive sides to how Big Tech's resources are used. Well-known tech companies are tackling challenging social and environmental issues caused by lack of consistent global regulation of internet technology and ease of criminals avoiding detection online. For an example of Big Tech working for the common good, we can look to 2018, when major technology companies agreed to work with World Wildlife Fund through the Global Coalition to End Wildlife Trafficking Online. Twenty-one companies including Alibaba, eBay, Etsy, Google, Instagram, Microsoft, Pinterest, Shengshi Collection, Tencent, and 58 Group pledged to work together to collectively reduce wildlife trafficking online across platforms by 80% by 2020 (WWF 2018). In collaboration with WWF, TRAFFIC, and the International Fund for Animal Welfare (IFAW), each company has been developing and implementing policies and solutions to help end wildlife trafficking online. According to WWF, bringing industry together offers the best opportunity to close the web to wildlife traffickers. Inconsistent policies and enforcement allow for trafficking ads to be removed from one site to pop up on another. Illegal sales run from elephant ivory carvings to live animals such as tiger cubs. Further, the sales are in breach of a site's rules. WWF finds that because the Internet's global connectivity and relative anonymity of sellers, combined with rapid transport, enable wildlife traffickers to buy, sell, and ship animals and wildlife products with an online transaction. There is a further worry that as traders and consumers move online, it will be critical to ensure that social media and e-commerce platforms cannot be exploited by the loopholes to detection created by wildlife traffickers (WWF 2018).

The estimated annual value of wildlife crime globally is $20 billion. Approximately 20,000 African elephants are illegally killed each year for trade in their tusks, and nearly three rhinos are poached each day in South Africa alone for their horns. WWF claims that countless species are under threat from trafficking, accelerated by online access to consumers, most of whom are unaware that the product they are buying could be devastating species populations and funding crime gangs (WWF 2018). This illustration shows the yin-yang of the impact of technology and the planet. According to the UN Intergovernmental Science-Policy Platform on Biodiversity and Ecosystem Services, wildlife protection is critical: more than 1 million species could be extinct within the next few decades (IPBES 2019).

But Big Tech's dark side can appear more pronounced than its contributions to social or environmental good. A 2020 edition of MIT Technology Review pointed out that Silicon Valley didn't equip the United States with the infrastructure and technology it needed to fight the COVID-19 pandemic. It hasn't provided many solutions to climate change. Its gig-economy platforms contribute to weakening labor protections, and its social media sites spread misinformation that weakens democracy (MIT Technology Review 2020). The dark side of Big Tech's impact on the world's most vulnerable is illustrated in a *Financial Times* headline: *Tech giants sued over child deaths in DRC cobalt mining* (Dempsey 2019). A landmark legal case was brought against the world's largest tech companies by families living in the Democratic Republic of the Congo (DRC) who say their children were killed or maimed while mining for cobalt used to power smartphones, laptops, and electric cars (Kelly 2019). Apple, Google, Dell, Microsoft, and Tesla were named as defendants. Cobalt is needed to power rechargeable lithium batteries used in millions of products sold by popular brand tech companies. Demand for products has tripled in the past five years and is expected to double again by the end of 2020. More than 60% of cobalt originates in DRC, one of the poorest and most unstable countries in the world (Kelly 2019).

The court papers allege that cobalt from the UK Glencore-owned mines is sold to Umicore, a Brussels-based metal and mining trader, which then sells battery-grade cobalt to Apple, Google, Tesla, Microsoft, and Dell. Other plaintiffs in the court documents say they worked at mines owned by Zhejiang Huayou Cobalt, a major Chinese cobalt firm which the lawsuit claims supplies Apple, Dell, and Microsoft and is likely to supply the other defendants.

Children were paid as little as $2 a day for dangerous work in which many were said to have died in tunnel collapses while others suffered life-changing injuries from accidents. The tech companies have been accused of being complicit in the forced child labor. Specifically, the families believe the tech companies had the authority and resources to supervise and regulate their cobalt supply chains, and they knew of the conditions and the link of their products to dangerous child labor conditions.

Apple responded saying: "In 2014, we were the first to start mapping our cobalt supply chain to the mine level and since 2016, we have published a full list of our identified cobalt refiners every year, 100 percent of which are participating in independent third-party audits. If a refiner is unable or unwilling to meet our standards, they will be removed from our supply chain. We've removed six cobalt refiners in 2019" (Kelly 2019). As the world's insatiable desire for tech products grow, the issue of slavery in the supply chain will remain a grave concern.

In this book, we do not want to downplay the dark side of Big Tech, and the current tensions are especially apparent in Chapter 5. At the same time, we do not want to overlook the "Tech for Good" entrepreneurs who are hoping technology will spur positive social change. Chapter 5 describes Big Finance and Big Tech prototypes that are being used for good. One is Humanity United The Working Capital Fund, which is an example of how large companies including Apple, Disney, and Walmart are partnering with Humanity United, Open Society, and Children's Investment Fund Foundation to use technology and business to address modern-day slavery in the supply chain. A second example in Chapter 6 is the USB's Educate Girls Development Impact Bond (DIB) which shows how big banks can use social finance for good and serve as a launch pad to advance the SDGs through partnerships with IdInsight and Educate Girls to more effectively target and scale education of girls' efforts through technology. Also, in Chapter 6, there is the Future-Fit Foundation case that captures how Big Tech and Big Finance can work together to take on Wicked Problems in a purposeful way.

What Is Social Finance?

The industry-wide definition of social finance is still evolving as academic literature and test cases help to shape the practical understanding of the field. There are no universal definitions for some common financial instruments used to pursue the SDGs (Weber and Ermotti 2018). We use two definitions of social finance. First is the one used at the Oxford Social Finance Programme, provided by Oxford scholar and *Social Finance* author Alex Nicholls et al. (2015): "The allocation of capital primarily for social and environmental returns, as well as in some cases, a financial return."

Social finance represents new investment approaches aimed at solving complex social challenges, and delivering social and environmental returns at below- or market-rate financial returns. As illustrated in Fig. 1.1, these investment tools encompass hybrid funding models and structured deals that blend various types of capital, from philanthropy to private capital. Funding can come from philanthropic donations, government grants,

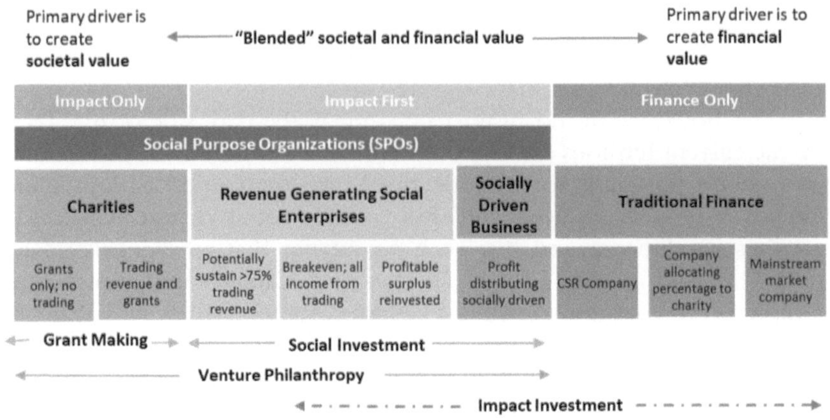

Fig. 1.1 Mapping social finance (*Source* Adapted from 2018 Global Impact Investors Network)

"soft" return debt and equity, mutual finance, or "finance first" and "total portfolio" impact investing strategies (Nicholls et al. 2015).

Social finance invites all investors to consider social improvement as an important value-add to society and to their organizations (Nicholls 2012).

Another definition of social finance is used by the UBS Optimus Foundation (Optimus) to leverage private capital: "Financial mechanisms that have potential to mobilize significant private funding for development programs, while increasing the effectiveness of such programs in solving the world's most pressing social challenges. Private capital is designed to complement and supplement, rather than replace, existing funding from governments and NGOs." To Optimus, social finance also means an "explicit intention to generate measurable social impact, alongside a (typically below-market) financial return" (The UBS Optimus Foundation 2018).

These two definitions of social finance are complemented by others from the broader field, such as the Social Affairs and Inclusion Directorate of the European Commission, which offers additional social finance characteristics: methods that are autonomous of the state, nominally repayable, transparent about social impact outcomes, and inclusive (Varga and Hayday 2016).

Who Are the Players in Social Finance?

The various actors involved in the social finance ecosystem fall into three main roles—demand, supply, and intermediators—as described in Fig. 1.2.

On the supply side, banks, governments, venture capitalists, community development agencies, and other funders provide up-front capital. From there, intermediaries allocate the funding to the on-the-ground service providers. These intermediaries sometimes also manage risk for supply-side investors. Demand-side players are often nonprofits, charities, and social purpose businesses that allocate services and goods to vulnerable individuals in target countries and regions. These groups are responsible for measuring and reporting results to show progress on specific social issues (Rexhepi 2017).

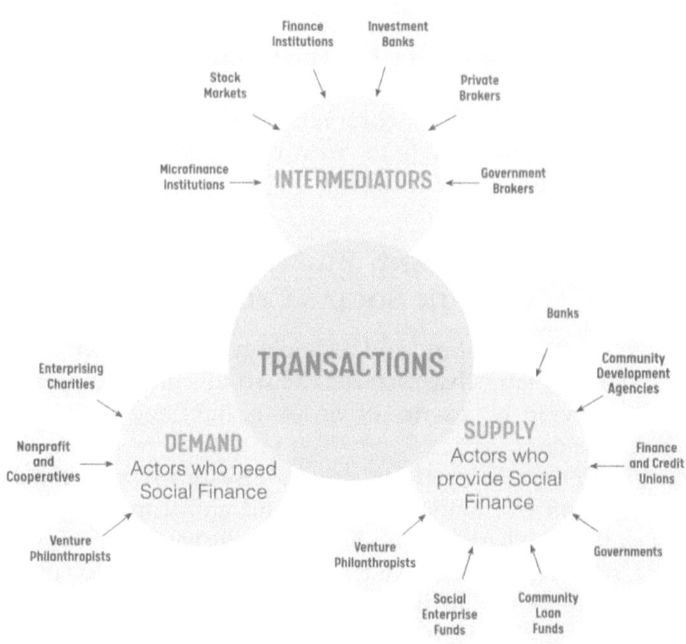

Fig. 1.2 Overview of social finance marketplace (*Source* Adapted and re-drawn from Gadaf Rexhepi [2017])

The Social Finance Movement

Social finance is becoming more than a method of investment—it's a movement fueled by growing client and CEO interests and the call for private sector support of the UN SDGs, which are uniting action across sectors for a common purpose (Nicholls et al. 2015; Christian et al. 2017). Attitudes across sectors are also changing about the definition of "impact and success," with a greater focus on programs that are business-oriented and evidence-based (The Global Impact Investing Network 2018). Education is crucial to building this movement. Partners for a New Economy (P4NE) have backed pfc social impact advisors' Capital for the Common Good Initiative which uses global online and in-classroom curricula, cases, and videos featuring alternative economic and financial models to train and transform social finance executives—current and future—to adopt new economic models that are human and planet-centric. The materials are used on the Oxford Social Finance course (Said Business School), and are being shared with 45 collaborating academic partners and the Skoll Centre for Entrepreneurship. In order to scale up their impact even further, they are also promoted to private and public sector colleagues so that they incorporate them into their own work so that their actions are more likely to reform the global economy in a way that allows people and nature to thrive.

Big Finance and Big Technology's Role in Social Change

Social finance, impact investing, and technology are often seen as panaceas to cure Wicked Problems that threaten the world's most vulnerable. This optimism is tempered by a series of yin-yang, light and dark side events over the past decade.

Several triggers are accelerating private investment in social change. First, the implosion of Lehman Brothers and global meltdown in 2008 triggered a shift in the banking and financial industry. The crisis continues to serve as a stark reminder of what can go wrong on a global scale and the enormous level of public distrust ignited toward financial institutions. It also spurred several banks to adopt more socially oriented products. (A jaded perspective is that the activity was an effort to improve their public image; the more positive perspective is that the crisis led to an epiphany that money has a greater social value.)

Regardless of the motivation, there have been several financial institutions that have made a commitment to what can be called "capital with purpose." CEOs like Blackrock's Larry Fink and Sergio Ermotti long-time CEO of UBS (now at Swiss Re) are calling for proactive leadership toward sustainability goals. UBS created its #TOGETHER public campaign that supports the SDGs. The year 2019 saw 181 business leaders of the Business Roundtable pass a new statement to redefine the purpose of a corporation as including all stakeholders—not just shareholders—but employees, community, customers, and suppliers (Business Roundtable 2019). Other examples of business' action to support social and environmental good include Goldman Sachs's acquisition of Imprint Capital in 2015, and the launch in 2019 of the Sustainable Finance Group. Schroders acquired Blue Orchard, a leading global impact investment manager, calling it "a blueprint for the future of our industry" (Schroders 2019). Such initiatives are part of a growing ecosystem of investors, asset managers, investees, advisers, and think tanks that expand the scope of social finance and what it means. Finance Innovation Lab, for instance, incubates new thinking, models, and leadership within the financial sector to put environmental sustainability at its core connects, and to facilitate a shift to a financial system that serves people and planet. There is also ongoing work to promote a shift in monetary policy so that the monetary and credit systems are aligned with ecological and social sustainability. For example, a group of think tanks—New Economics Foundation, Council on Economic Policies, Institute for Innovation and Public Purpose at University College London—are collaborating to leverage the influential position of central banks in financial markets so they use their own balance sheets to support environmental objectives; to steer private sector financing toward sustainable investments; and to significantly reduce financial flows to unsustainable economic activities.

Collaboration and partnership are a recurring aspect of capital with purpose initiatives. Climate Safe Lending, for instance, is an action-focused network of banks and bank influencers—including institutional investors, insurance companies, and civil society leaders—that seeks to redirect bank credit toward climate safe activities. It seeks to align European and North American bank lending with the goals of the Paris Climate Accord to keep the planet well below a 1.5° Celsius temperature rise, and hosts a peer-learning lab for internal leaders at medium- to large-size banks. It offers methodologies, models, tools, insights, and other enabling mechanisms to more rapidly accelerate climate positive lending in their institutions; and a coordinated effort among banks and bank influencers to directly engage banks to move along five progressive levels of balance sheet decarbonization.

Some critics dismiss efforts involving Big Finance as window dressing by an industry that still invests the majority of its holdings in traditional, non-sustainable ways. There have been clear examples of Big Finance masquerading as social purpose. An exposé by the *Wall Street Journal* found The Abraaj Group, a private equity firm, misused funds purchasing yachts and living a luxury lifestyle, while the founder received high marks for building his firm's social mission and speaking at high-profile events such as the World Economic Forum's (WEF) Davos about the role of private equity in supporting social good (Clark 2019). The firm proclaimed it could achieve triple bottom line results but was found to have mismanaged its $1bn healthcare fund. Dubai-based Abraaj had dominated the emerging markets private equity sector. Social purpose funds mostly came from large institutional investors, including the Bill & Melinda Gates Foundation.

It will take time and a concerted effort to ensure that investments with integrity are measurable and that high industry ethics are greeted as the norm. Positive Money is a research and campaigning organization that seeks to reform the banking system, especially the central banks. Positive Money works to align central bank policy with sustainability by advocating for the Bank of England, the Bank of France and the European Central Bank to disclose the carbon footprint of their balance sheets and to add sustainability to their mandates and monetary policy frameworks.

Perhaps there is good news that young people and women investors are ready to hold business accountable and call on investment firms to "up their game," making a commitment to evidenced-based social finance. Gen Z and X and women clients of all ages continue to demand investments in their portfolios achieve social and environmental returns. Annual surveys undertaken by Deloitte, RBC Wealth Management, and Morgan Stanley all show similar trends. Young clients worldwide believe their investments can positively impact climate change and poverty. RBC finds that 86% of younger Asians believe they have more opportunity to tackle societal issues through investing, compared with 67% of youth in the West (The Economist Intelligence Unit 2018). Morgan Stanley research shows that 75% of millennials surveyed believed their investments could positively impact climate change and 84% believe their investments could move people out of poverty (Choi 2018). A Deloitte survey shows four in ten millennials believe business has a negative impact on society and the environment, and that business is not doing enough to change behavior (Deloitte 2017).

At the same time, there is growing use of environmental, social, and governance (ESG) factors as a proxy for doing good, even though there is inconsistency in how these principles are interpreted across the financial industry and the positive impact they have. RBC's Managing Director, Tom Van Dyck, in the San Francisco office is expanding RBC's profile and commitment to ESG and sustainable investments, and we will discuss his experiences in Chapter 3. He is part of a growing community of theorists and practitioners that is reimagining some of the basic premises and beliefs about the economy and financial success. This includes a new generation of economists—especially women—who are upending their field by questioning the meaning of everything from "value" and "debt" to "growth" and "GDP." They include people such as Kate Raworth whose work on "doughnut economics" asks that we measure economic success in terms of how social and economic activity adds social and environmental value, and enables people to live within the limits of planetary boundaries. Mariana Mazzucato takes aim at the concept of value, arguing that to date what is rewarded is value extraction rather than value creation. Carlota Perez, Esther Duflo, and Stephanie Kelton are among the other economists offering alternative theories to the long-established but increasingly questioned ones that highlighted shareholder value, financial performance, and economic growth. (See Chapter 1 References for examples of these 'new economists' works.)

Meanwhile, technology too is reshaping our economy, our institutions, and our relationships. Big Tech is spawning what the World Economic Forum (WEF) calls the Fourth Industrial Revolution, which has significant opportunities and challenges: "technology will lead to a supply-side miracle, with long-term gains in efficiency and productivity. Transportation and communication costs will drop, logistics and global supply chains will become more effective, and the cost of trade will diminish, all of which will open new markets and drive economic growth." But the WEF also predicts that this technology "miracle" could expand global inequality, one of the greatest societal concerns today and in the future. This "winner-takes-all" technology-based economy stagnates incomes and hollows out the middle class (Schwab 2016). The rapid rise in unemployment due to the COVID-19 pandemic showed just how vulnerable many jobs are and how susceptible global economic systems can be to rapid shocks.

For all of its gains, the dark side of technology companies continues to come to life. Most high profile were the revelations of Facebook and Cambridge Analytica's intrusion into the US 2016 election (Cadwalladr and Graham-Harrison 2018). The pernicious influence of YouTube in the election of populist candidates around the world, like Brazil's Jair Bolsonaro, illustrates a growing dangerous and seemingly unchecked trend in social media and technologies' political influence (Fisher and Taub 2019). The Council on Foreign Affairs cites that social media is spawning hate speech and violence against immigrants and helping expand global right-wing populist politics leading to the erosion of democracy and expansion of autocracy and dictatorship (Laub 2019).

The adaptation of technology from the private to the social sphere raises important questions and lessons for the field of social finance: What features of technology (both positive and negative) are replicated when a commercial technology model is repositioned in a social setting? How can those implementing technology for social finance goals ensure that the interests of vulnerable communities are heard and represented in solutions? What do social change and technology experts need to know about each other's fields? What is the role of different forms of capital in accelerating creative solutions across these fields? And what leadership practices are needed to address the Wicked Problems emanating from sociotechnical induced changes?

Author Peter Townsend points to concerns that good ideas and intentions can produce undesirable results that threaten human survival (Townsend 2016). He says, "Progress is often transient, as faster electronics and computers dramatically shorten retention of data, knowledge, and information loss. Progress and globalization are also destroying past language and cultures .... Similarly, progress of electronics and communication has produced a boom industry in cybercrime and cyberterrorism .... Over enthusiasm in creating a global food economy is devastating the environment and causing extinction of species, just to support an excessive human population." Curbing the dark side will require planning, investment, and political commitment. Townsend's warning is stark: "Failure to respond implies human extinction" (Townsend 2016).

Sustainable Development Goals: Solving the World's Wicked Problems

More money is needed to respond to the challenges raised by Townsend, and it is increasingly concentrated at the top. Oxfam reports the rich keep getting richer. In 2018, billionaire fortunes increased by 12%—or US$2.5 billion a day—while the 3.8 billion people who make up the poorest half of humanity saw their wealth decline by 11% (Lawson et al. 2019). There is a dangerous, growing gap between rich and poor that is undermining the fight against poverty, damaging our economies, and fueling public anger across the globe. According to the Oxfam report, "governments are exacerbating inequality by underfunding public services, such as health care and education, on the one hand, while under taxing corporations and the wealthy, and failing to clamp down on tax dodging, on the other." Women and girls bear the brunt of inequality and are the hardest hit by its impact on health, education, and economic opportunity (Lawson et al. 2019). For example, an estimated 40 million people, 70% of whom are women, are victims of modern slavery. Approximately 25 million are victims of forced labor, which yields $51 billion in illicit profits annually (Boundless Impact Investing, 2018). Increased globalization, labor outsourcing, and intense market competition in industries such as fast fashion, have created complex and exploitative supply chains across the world. Combined with complex drivers of poverty, gender, caste, and migrant status, these often opaque and untraceable supply chains allow worker exploitation and abuse on the factory floors of multinational corporations. It is too early to know the impact of the COVID-19 pandemic on poverty, but the early indications are that not only have poor people in all countries been the most affected regardless of geography, but it is pushing millions of people back into extreme poverty with predictions that poverty levels will slip back to 2016 levels (World Bank 2020).

Concurrently, climate change can no longer be treated as hypothetical. The World Bank estimates that 143 million climate refugees will migrate from three regions (Latin America, sub-Saharan Africa, and Southeast Asia) by 2050 (Rigaud et al. 2018). They will be driven by the onset of desertification, flooding, forest fires, droughts, and intensified storms. And climate change doesn't operate in isolation. Slavery, for instance, has a climate change connection. According to academic activist Kevin Bales, slavery is the cause of much of the natural world's destruction. Bales puts slavery in this context, “If slavery were an American state it would have the population of California, the economic output of the District of Columbia, but it would be the world’s third-largest producer of CO_2, after China and the United States” (Bales 2016).

These kinds of challenge elide to create some of the world’s most Wicked Problems. Wicked Problems are the big, complex, and dynamic challenges society confronts. Many of their components are captured in the United Nations (UN) Sustainable Development Goals (SDGs) which provide a broad overview of issues that need to be addressed by 2030. There are seventeen SDGs, and together they summarize the daunting real-life challenges facing humanity—challenges that include poverty, inequality, modern-day slavery, climate change, protection of oceans and forests and indigenous people (UNDP 2017).

Table 1.1 lists the goals and provides examples of the indicators that international bodies and national governments have promised to meet, and to which other organizations such as business have signed up to. There are arguments about whether or not the SDGs—and particularly the indicators—are too ambitious, or are so broad that institutions can cherry-pick ones that are easy while ignoring ones that might be more impactful. However, for the purposes of this book, the SDGs provide a broad overview of what social finance should be aiming to address, and the areas Big Tech and Big Finance should be targeting. What the SDGs also provide is a chart for understanding the many components of sustainability, and how when they come together they can create problems that are confusing and contradictory. These are known as Wicked Problems, and understanding what they are is central to how social finance should advance sustainable development among the world’s poor.

What Are Wicked Problems?

Google search the term Wicked Problems and it reveals 55,300,000 results in 0.63 seconds. It is a term and framework that has been adopted and used by scholars, policymakers, and urban and social designers worldwide since the 1960s. What makes a problem wickedly difficult? Complexity. Wicked Problems are difficult to understand, and are often a symptom of another problem with interrelated issues—pull one thread and many others may unravel.

Oxford scholar Steve Rayner (2006) described Wicked Problems as “characteristics of deeper problems.” For example, climate change, like

Table 1.1 Sustainable Development Goals

Goal	*Sample indicator*	*Goal*	*Sample indicator*
No-poverty	By 2030, eradicate extreme poverty for all people everywhere, currently measured as people living on less than $1.25 a day	Industry, innovation, and infrastructure	By 2020, substantially reduce the proportion of youth not in employment, education, or training
Zero hunger	By 2030, end hunger and ensure access by all people to safe, nutritious, and sufficient food all year round	Reduced inequality	Develop quality, reliable, sustainable, and resilient infrastructure with a focus on affordable and equitable access for all
Good health and well-being	By 2030, reduce the global maternal mortality ratio to less than 70 per 100,000 live births	Sustainable cities and communities	By 2030, ensure access for all to adequate, safe, and affordable housing and basic services and upgrade slums
Quality education	By 2030, ensure that all youth and a substantial proportion of adults, both men and women, achieve literacy and numeracy	Responsible consumption and production	By 2030, substantially reduce waste generation through prevention, reduction, recycling, and reuse
Gender equality	Eliminate all harmful practices, such as child, early and forced marriage, and female genital mutilation	Climate action	Integrate climate change measures into national policies, strategies, and planning
Clean water and sanitation	By 2020, protect and restore water-related ecosystems, including mountains, forests, wetlands, rivers, aquifers, and lakes	Life below water	Provide access for small-scale artisanal fishers to marine resources and markets

(continued)

Table 1.1 (continued)

Goal	*Sample indicator*	*Goal*	*Sample indicator*
Affordable and clean energy	By 2030, double the global rate of improvement in energy efficiency	Life on land	Mobilize and significantly increase financial resources from all sources to conserve and sustainably use biodiversity and ecosystems
Decent work and economic growth	By 2020, substantially reduce the proportion of youth not in employment, education, or training	Peace, justice, and strong institutions	Significantly reduce all forms of violence and related death rates everywhere
Partnerships to achieve the goal	Mobilize additional financial resources for developing countries from multiple sources		

educational underperformance or food insecurity, "has a kind of circularity that goes on, the same things crop up as explanations of other parts of the problem. Wherever you push, it pops out somewhere else" (Rayner 2006). Climate change is connected to poverty, is connected to deforestation, is connected to indigenous rights, is connected to economic development, and so on. There is a web of issues and stakeholders that must be recognized and understood when tackling complex challenges.

Wicked Problems are also unique to the circumstances and context. Though enormous progress can be made in alleviating Wicked Problems, they will likely remain with us—child abuse, domestic violence, and poverty are examples. The search for solutions and strategies to mitigate them is ongoing (Stichler 2009). They require skillful, courageous leaders to tame them.

A History of Wicked Problems

Academic Horst W. J. Rittel started talking about Wicked Problems in the mid-1960s (Skaburskis 2008) to describe "that class of problems which are ill-formulated, where the information is confusing, where there are many decision makers and clients with conflicting values, and where the ramifications in the whole system are confusing" (Churchman 1967). In 1972 Wicked Problems were described in the publication, "On the Planning Crisis: Systems Analysis of the First and Second Generation" (Rittel 1972). In 1973, Rittel and Melvin M. Webber came out with their landmark article "Dilemmas in the General Theory of Planning" (Rittel and Webber 1973) in reflection of the complexity of the era, one of the most volatile periods of US history: racial violence unleashed by the deaths of Martin Luther King, Jr. and Malcolm X; massive student protests over the Vietnam War; the war on poverty publicly calling out the dichotomy of wealth and extreme poverty in America; environmental and public health crises over the use of cancer-causing pesticides such as DDT and defoliant Agent Orange; the 1973 oil crisis; and the nightly news reflecting the shattering of traditional boundaries of race, religion, and justice (Peterson 2010).

Rittel and Webber used the term Wicked Problems to name the social conditions of the times. As planners and social policy professionals, they recognized that a linear, scientific approach to problem-solving would not capture the colliding of complex systems (Peterson 2010). For example, the "Newtonian mechanisms" that had succeeded in solving the problems of the previous century—drinkable water, municipal sanitation, infectious diseases—would not sum up the nuance or tumult of contemporary concerns over equity and pluralism (Peterson 2010). Through Wicked Problems, Webber and Rittel found a way to describe the "waves of repercussions" that rippled through systemic networks of changing values and goals in a nation in turmoil (Rittel 1972).

Wicked Problems, as envisioned by Rittel and Webber (1973), captured the multidimensional nature of systems and allowed planners and policy professionals to describe the challenges they faced, "whether concerns over the location of a freeway, the adjustment of a tax rate, the modification of school curriculum, the confrontation of crime ... or The System ... as an evil source of misery and suffering" (Rittel and Webber 1973). The fathers of "Wicked" identified ten characteristics to identify Wicked Problems:

1. There is no definitive formulation of a Wicked Problem. It is impossible to write a well-defined problem statement about Wicked Problems.
2. Wicked Problems have no stopping rule. Since you cannot define the problem, it is difficult to tell when it is resolved.

3. Solutions to Wicked Problems are not true-or-false but good-or-bad: Choosing a solution to a Wicked Problem is a matter of judgment.
4. There is no immediate and no ultimate test of a solution to a Wicked Problem. Solutions to Wicked Problems generate waves of consequences, and it is impossible to know how all of the consequences will eventually play out. Measurement is hard.
5. Every implemented solution to a Wicked Problem has consequences: Solutions to Wicked Problems have consequences that cannot be undone.
6. Wicked Problems do not have a well-described set of potential solutions: Various stakeholders will have differing views of acceptable solutions. It is a matter of judgment as to when enough potential solutions have emerged, and which should be pursued. Wicked Problems do not have an exhaustively describable set of potential solutions.
7. Every Wicked Problem is essentially unique. There are no "classes" of solutions that can be applied to a specific case.
8. Every Wicked Problem can be considered a symptom of another problem: A Wicked Problem is a set of interlocking issues and constraints which change over time, embedded in a dynamic social context. They have no single root cause.
9. The causes of a Wicked Problem can be explained in numerous ways: There are many stakeholders who will have various and changing ideas about what might be a problem, what might be causing it, and how to resolve it.
10. A designer attempting to solve a Wicked Problem must be fully responsible for their actions. Problem solvers dealing with a wicked issue are held liable for the consequences of any actions.

Since the introduction of the Wicked Problems concept, it has been adapted and used across disciplines. Many scholars believe this "Disciplinarity"—knowledge creation that is transdisciplinary, reflective, nonlinear, and hybridized—has made the Wicked Problem framework useful and important (Yawson 2009). Use of the Wicked Problem framework is well documented by academics: public administration, political science, and public policy (Briggs 2007; Fischer 1993; Harmon and Mayer 1986; Head 2008, 2010; Roberts 2000), natural resource management and urban and regional planning (Allen and Gould 1986; Freeman 2000;

Innes and Booher 1999, 2016), cybernetics research (Conklin 2006), software engineering (DeGrace and Stahl 1990), interaction design (Stolterman 2008), military science (Clemente and Evans 2015), systems engineering (Kovacic and Sousa-Poza 2013), architectural design (Fischer et al. 1991), environmental policy (Balint et al. 2011), healthcare (Arnett 2012), management science (Dunne and Martin 2006), and organizational development (Marshak 2008; Fyke and Buzzanell 2013; Sherman and Peterson 2009; Ritchey 2011; Yawson 2015).

Over the years, scholars have added their own twist to Wicked Problems. Bayard Catron (1981) created key attributes of the Wicked Problem concept and taming wicked problems as *ontological* for identifying the existence of Wicked Problems, *epistemological* for challenging our ability to understand them, and *axiological* for questioning our ability to act rightly in relation to them.

Chaos theory, complexity theory, and complex adaptive practice are all ecosystem models underlining Wicked Problems framework (Peterson et al., 2018). Complexity theories tend to focus on systems and the interactions within them. These systems may be natural such as climate or they may be primarily human such as poverty. These theories maintain that "relationships in complex systems, like organizations, are made up of interconnections and branching choices that produce unintended consequences and render the universe unpredictable" (Tetenbaum 1998).

The unpredictable nature of Wicked Problems and the potential for unintended consequences is significant. To our team, the tenth characteristic describe by Rittel and Webber, is one of the most important: "A designer attempting to solve a Wicked Problem must be fully responsible for their actions. Problem solvers dealing with a wicked issue are held liable for the consequences of any actions." Being accountable for actions and doing no harm must be an ethical cornerstone for social investors. "Not knowing what you don't know" or placing "big bets"—a gambling metaphor popular among philanthropists and social investors to describe a willingness to take bold risks for high potential results—doesn't exonerate social investors from being liable for actions. Approaching social change as a high-risk game, could be a particularly dangerous as newcomers from finance and technology enter into the dynamic field of social and environmental change.

Although more business and engineering schools are teaching Wicked Problems, complexity and systems change, often this knowledge isn't fully incorporated into required curriculum and is considered an elective. Consequently, products of our schools are often unprepared to tackle Wicked Problems in practice. These complex challenges require skills different from those provided by traditional business schools such as training in empathy, inclusion, work-life balance, and knowledge of social justice and individual rights. To address the needs of a new workforce, *Fast Company* calls on companies to hire staff with Social Work degrees to help them build more ethical workplaces. Facebook, Uber, Wells Fargo have all apologized for corporate malfeasance that potentially could have benefitted from staff with training in social justice (Bullinger 2018).

A frequently used example of unintended consequences involves the Bill & Melinda Gates Foundation (Gates or Gates Foundation) efforts to reduce deaths from malaria worldwide. The Wicked Problem: there are an estimated 584,000 deaths from malaria worldwide, with 90% occurring in Sub-Saharan Africa. Nearly 300,000 children under the age of five died of malaria in 2016, equivalent to nearly 800 young lives lost each day. An estimated 200,000 infants die due to malaria during pregnancy. These deaths are preventable, by controlling human exposure to the mosquitos carrying the disease. For more than a decade, the Gates Foundation has tried to eradicate malaria and reduce deaths from the disease using a variety of strategies. One of the most high-profile strategies has been the widespread distribution of malaria nets in Africa (World Health Organization 2018).

In 2015 the *New York Times* reported on Gates' Malaria Net Initiative and the complexity of the problems associated with malaria deaths and the unintended consequences of the wholesale distribution of millions of mosquito nets (Gettleman 2015). A video documented the challenges and negative impacts on people and the environment. The title of the story captures the challenge: "Meant to Keep Malaria Out; Nets are Used to Haul Fish In: millions of mosquito nets are given out fight to malaria in Africa, yet many faced with hunger use them as fish nets, creating potential environmental problems." The story points out the dichotomy and tough decisions when poor people must make choices between hunger and health and destruction of life-sustaining fisheries and potential poisoning of people and fisheries with pesticide laced nets.

While using malaria nets for fishing may seem harmless, but the small holes of the nets needed to keep mosquitos away from humans are so small that they don't allow fish fry-lings to escape. The results: fishing nets decimated fisheries in communities across African countries including

Nigeria, Zambia, Tanzania, Mozambique, Uganda, Kenya, and Madagascar. The research illustrates the collateral damage done at scale, by one of the "biggest and most celebrated public health campaigns" in the world. Mosquito nets are a billion-dollar industry, with hundreds of millions of insecticide-treated nets being given away throughout Africa. While lives are being saved, the incidence of malaria deaths appears to be on the rise. According to World Malaria Report, there were 219 million cases of malaria in 2017, up from 217 million cases in 2016 (World Health Organization 2018).

Scientists are alarmed that the nets could imperil already stressed fish populations, a critical food source for millions of the world's poorest people. Governments have tried to prevent the use of nets by fisherman. The pesticides used on the nets are also dragged through lakes and rivers used as drinking supplies for residents. Permethrin is often used to treat the nets and is highly toxic to fish. Warnings that the nets should not be washed in a lake or river are frequently unnoticed or ignored.

There are concerns that the nets pose health risks to humans as well, although there is dispute about how significant this is. Fish can absorb the pesticides, and people then ingest them. Academic Anthony Hay calls the problem, "white man's burden" he believes, "We think we have a solution to everyone's problems and here is an example of where we're creating a new problem" (Gettleman 2015). Fortunately, the Gates Foundation has shifted to become more systems, community-oriented after learning about the unanticipated negative consequences of malaria nets. Avoiding arrogance and entering into deals with eyes wide open will be discussed in Chapter 2 on Deliberate Leadership.

Unintended consequences and taking responsibility for mistakes as social investors is essential. Wicked Problems will be with us forever, social investors will struggle and fall. Adaptation is essential. One of the ways to anticipate negative and positive outcomes is to understand the systemic nature of a problem. Our team uses the United Nations Development Programme (UNDP) human security framework to explain the interconnected nature of a Wicked Problem. These eight dimensions to identify what humans need to have "freedom from want and freedom from fear" as illustrated by Fig. 1.3

To help create questions for social investors to ask about potential negative and positive consequences, we converted the Human Security dimensions into a matrix Fig. 1.4. This approach allows investors to ask the questions—do we have sufficient information to understand

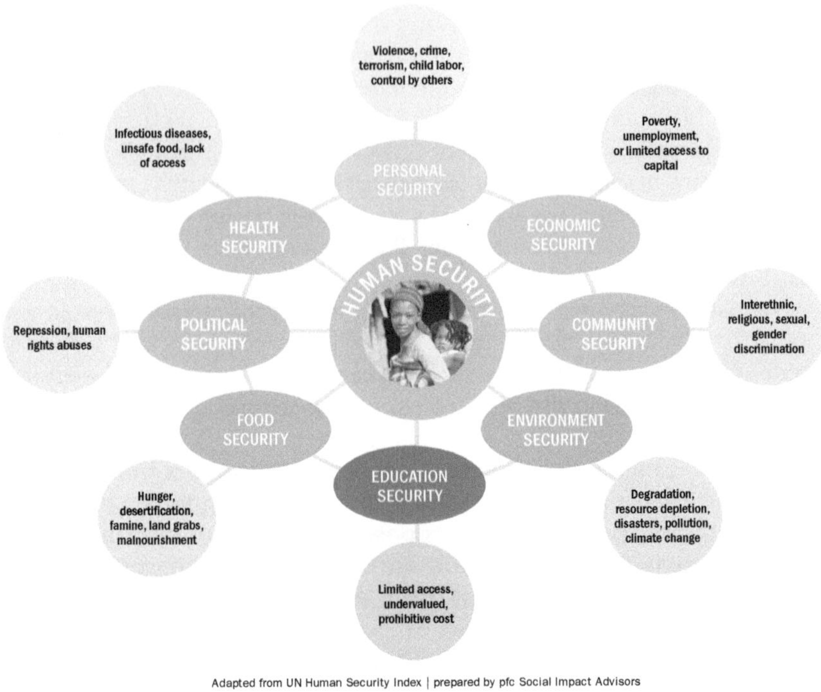

Fig. 1.3 UN Human Security Framework (*Source* Adapted from UN Development Programme, 1994 by pfc social impact advisors [Reproduced with permission from pfc social impact advisors, llc])

whether the investment will have a negative, positive, neutral, or harm. This approach allows investors who are unfamiliar with systemic social challenges to begin to see the system in action.

Is a Problem Wicked: The Taxonomy of Wicked Problems

To differentiate types of problems—and appropriate responses to these challenges—scholar Keith Grint (2010) created a taxonomy of problems to illustrate: Tame, Critical, and Wicked. Tame problems are generally linear, and solution can be managed: what Grint describes as déjà vu. Tame problems are known problems with known solutions that are within existing expertise and know how. *Tame problems* are best approached from a management style of leadership, with a structured logical approach: "I have seen this problem before and I can use the same strategies to solve

	POSITIVE	NEGATIVE	NEUTRAL	NEED MORE INFO
PERSONAL: Violence, crime, terrorism, child labor, control by others	☐	☐	☐	☐
ECONOMIC: Poverty, unemployment, no access to capital	☐	☐	☐	☐
COMMUNITY: Interethnic, religious, sexual, or gender discrimination	☐	☐	☐	☐
ENVIRONMENT: Degradation, resource depletion, disasters, pollution, climate change	☐	☐	☐	☐
EDUCATION: Limited access, undervalued, prohibitive cost	☐	☐	☐	☐
FOOD: Hunger, famine, desertification, malnourishment, obesity, land grabs	☐	☐	☐	☐
POLITICAL: Repression, human rights abuses	☐	☐	☐	☐
HEALTH: Infectious diseases, unsafe food, lack of access to healthcare	☐	☐	☐	☐

Adapted from UN Human Security Index | prepared by pfc Social Impact Advisors

Fig. 1.4 Human Security Framework and unintended consequences matrix (*Source* Adapted from UN Human Security Index | prepared by social impact advisors [Reproduced with permission from pfc social impact advisors llc])

it as I have in the past." Examples include life-saving heart surgery or building a complex bridge.

Critical problems cause a crisis and need immediate action. They demand immediate and decisive actions or "command and control." They fetch uncertainty and fear. "Commanders" are needed who will coerce people into action and tell people what to do. Examples include a fire or an automobile accident.

Wicked problems are complex problems that hold a multitude of other problems within them. There is no known solution. Sometimes they have to be accepted and adapted to rather than overcome. Wicked Problems require a different type of leadership: "I have not seen this problem before and the challenges I face require me to think and act differently." Leaders need to embrace collaboration and invite new and divergent perspectives to the table to help offer new approaches to problem-solving. They also require leaders to be empathetic, to listen and to "walk in someone's shoes."

Wicked Problems represent complex social, environmental, and organizational challenges such as the SDGs, and change is based on the lens through which leaders view the problem over time. Academic Peter Senge (2006)—senior lecturer at the MIT Sloan School of Management and founder of the Society for Organizational Learning—and author of the seminal book, *The Fifth Discipline: The Art and Practice of the Learning Organization*, distinguishes between two types of complexity as "detail complexity" and "dynamic complexity." The complexity of Wicked Problems is dynamic and "cause and effect are distant in time and space"; whereas complexity associated with tame problems is detailed, and although there are many variables, they are predictable (Yawson 2015).

Like Grint, Harvard professor Ronald Heifetz (1994) also categorizes problems into three types. He describes Type I situations as technical, where the problem can be defined and can be solved with an engineering know-how and skills. Type II situations are where the problem is apparent, but the solution is not. Type III situations are adaptive problems, where there are no obvious definitions of the problem or the solution. Type I problems are tame or technical problems and can be very complex, but they are not messy and have a readily available solution (Heifetz et al. 2009). Types II and III are complex, multi-framed, cross-boundary, hard to solve, and are Wicked Problems (Yawson 2015). Heifetz (1994) explains that Types II and III are increasingly becoming problems that organizations face and thus call for "new leadership skills and competencies, a dynamic process that emphasizes the need for quality, flexibility, adaptability, speed, and experimentation" (Beinecke 2009).

Climate change has introduced unprecedented complexity and jeopardy into the world. It has a rapid and devastating domino effect, especially on the poor. The strategies for tackling climate will require radical innovation and transformation to protect very vulnerable people and planet. There are no quick wins or simple solutions (Catron 1981). A path forward will require collaboration across stakeholders that are often mired in disagreement (Beinecke 2009). Moreover, finding solutions will be difficult to recognize because of the complex interdependencies of government, business, and civil society organizations (Connolly and Stanfield 2006).

Steven Rayner summarized these challenges, "we are not dealing with problems where we're just uncertain, we're dealing with problems where people know what the answer is. Different people know what the answer is. The trouble is the answers they have are just irreconcilable with each other" (Rayner 2006). Reconciling these diverse options and opinions requires decentralized power and leaders able to successfully navigate tough negotiations. Wicked Problems may be best tamed by identifying "preferred directions" rather than "optimal solutions" (Catron 1981). Leaders taking on Wicked Problems must be bricoleurs—French for jack-of-all trades—uniquely crafting solutions (or cobbling them together) using the appropriate tools for the problem—whether command and control, managed, or adaptive leadership, or a combination of them all. French social anthropologist Claude Lévi-Strauss described the process of bricolage as the artist who "shapes the beautiful and useful out of the dump heap of human life." He compared the artistic process to the work of a handyman who solves technical or mechanical problems with whatever materials are available.

Global leaders today must be very talented at bricolage to succeed against Wicked Problems. Annually, the WEF publishes its Global Risk Report, and in 2020 the top ten challenges that keep an estimated 1000 cross-sectorial leaders awake at night include: extreme weather conditions; failure of climate change mitigation and adaptation; natural and man-made environmental disasters; biodiversity loss and ecosystem collapse; water crises; cyber-attacks and data fraud; global governance failure; and large scale involuntary migration. If the report had come out a few months later, infectious diseases would most certainly have been added to that list. Again, these are issues and leadership skills that are not typically taught in business schools. Overall, Big Finance and Big Technology leaders are unprepared for tackling the Medusa-like, large scale global problem. They must navigate global negotiations that are entwined in politics and diverse opinions of business, advocates, and government. It will require, in the words of Richard Pascale, world leaders who will need to "act their way into a new way of thinking" (Pascale et al. 2001, p. 229).

Conclusion

Big Technology and Big Finance are so pervasive in modern life that it seems inevitable expectations are placed on them that go beyond shareholder value and legal compliance. One of the ways they can add new types of value is when they come together in the field of social finance. Social finance is not only made possible because of advances in technology, it is increasingly important given the array of interrelated Wicked Problems affecting people's lives and planetary well-being.

However, money and technology alone can't resolve Wicked Problems. The complexity of the world's most intractable problems requires individual and organizational leadership that is fearless, compassionate, and adaptive. Because each Wicked Problem is unique, leaders must choose their approaches carefully. Should they employ command and control decisions when faced with a crisis? Should they manage the problem by calling on previous successful experiences? When facing a complex challenge, should they be collaborative and adaptive leaders, adjusting their strategy based on clear-eyed understanding of what is and is not working? How do leaders hold onto their vision while putting their preconceived notions aside, recognizing the strengths and limits of their expertise and seeking solutions where one might least expect to find them, including across disciplines and within communities affected by the problem?

To answer these questions we will now introduce Deliberate Leadership, an amalgam of the most effective adaptive leadership strategies as a framework to empower leaders in social finance and impact investing to thoughtful take on complex problems and accept the risk and consequences of decision-making and the challenges ahead. On to Chapter 2.

References

Allen, G.M., and E.M. Gould. 1986. Complexity, Wickedness and Public Forests. *Journal of Forestry* 84 (4): 20–24.

Arnett, Donna K. 2012. Wicked Problems and Worthy Pursuits. *Circulation* 125 (21) (May 29): 2554–2556.

Bales, Kevin. 2016. *Blood and Earth: Modern Slavery, Ecocide, and the Secret to Saving the World*. New York, NY: Spiegel & Grau.

Balint, P.J., R.E. Stewart, A. Desai, and L.C. Walters. 2011. *Wicked Environmental Problems: Managing Uncertainty and Conflict*. Washington, DC: Springer/Island Press.

Beinecke, Richard H. 2009. Introduction: Leadership for Wicked Problems. *The Innovation Journal: The Public Sector Innovation* 14 (1): 1–17.

Briggs, L. 2007. Tackling Wicked Problems: A Public Policy Perspective. Barton ACT: Australian Public Service Commission (APSC).

Brondizio, E., J. Settele, S. Díaz, and H. T. Ngo (eds.). 2019. Global Assessment Report on Biodiversity and Ecosystem Services of the Intergovernmental Science-Policy Platform on Biodiversity and Ecosystem Services, November. IPBES Secretariat, Bonn, Germany.

Bullinger, Jake. 2018. Why Companies Need to Hire Social Workers. *Fast Company*, June 20.

Business Roundtable. 2019. Statement on the Purpose of a Corporation, August 25. Business Roundtable.

Cadwalladr, Carole, and Emma Graham-Harrison. 2018. Revealed: 50 Million Facebook Profiles Harvested for Cambridge Analytica in Major Data Breach. *The Guardian*, March 17.

Catron, Bayard L. 1981. On Taming Wicked Problems. *Dialogue* 3 (3): 13–16.

Choi, Audrey. 2018. How Younger Investors Could Reshape the World. Morgan Stanley. https://www.morganstanley.com/access/why-millennial-investors-are-different.

Christian, Petroske, Florian Parzhuber, Haneol Jeong, John Kinsella, Maaya Murakami, Mitchell Laferriere, and Remi Cordelle. 2017. SoFi 101: Understanding Social Finance. *Social Space*, 8–14.

Churchman, C. West. 1967. Guest Editorial: Wicked Problems. *Management Science* 14 (4): B141–B142.

Clark, Simon. 2019. Abraaj Founder Arif Naqvi Accused of Misappropriating More Than $250 Million in New Indictment. *The Wall Street Journal*, June 13.

Clemente, Dave, and Ryan Evans. 2015. *Wartime Logistics in Afghanistan and Beyond: Analyzing Complex Adaptive Systems as Networks and as Wicked Problems*. London, UK: Royal Institute for International Affairs/Chatham House.

Conklin, Jeff. 2006. Wicked Problems and Social Complexity. In *Dialogue Mapping: Building Understanding of Wicked Problems*, ed. Jeff Conklin. Hoboken, NJ: John Wiley.

Connolly, Thomas, and Mark Stanfield. 2006. Using Games-Based ELearning Technologies in Overcoming Difficulties in Teaching Information Systems. *Journal of Information Technology Education* 5: 459–476.

DeGrace, Peter, and Leslie Hulet Stahl. 1990. *Wicked Problems, Righteous Solutions: A Catalog of Modern Engineering Paradigms*. Upper Saddle River, NJ: Prentice Hall.

Deloitte. 2017. The 2017 Deloitte Millennial Survey.

Dempsey, Harry. 2019. Tech Giants Sued Over Child Deaths in DRC Cobalt Mining. *Financial Times*, December 16.

Dunne, David, and Roger Martin. 2006. Design Thinking and How It Will Change Management Education: An Interview and Discussion. *Academy of Management Learning & Education* 5 (4): 512–523. https://doi.org/10.5465/amle.2006.23473212.

Fink, Larry. 2019. A Sense of Purpose. BlackRock.

Fischer, F. 1993. Citizen Participation and the Democratization of Policy Expertise: From Theoretical Inquiry to Practical Cases. *Policy Sciences* 26 (1): 163–187.

Fischer, Gerhard, Andreas C. Lemke, Raymond McCall, and Anders I. Morch. 1991. Making Argumentation Serve Design. *Human-Computer Interaction* 6 (3–4): 393–419.

Fisher, Max, and Amanda Taub. 2019. How YouTube Radicalized Brazil. *The New York Times,* August 11.

Freeman, David M. 2000. Wicked Water Problems: Sociology and Local Water Organizations in Addressing Water Resources Policy. *Journal of the American Water Resources Association* 36 (3): 483–491.

Fyke, Jeremy P., and Patrice M. Buzzanell. 2013. The Ethics of Conscious Capitalism: Wicked Problems in Leading Change and Changing Leaders. *Human Relations* 66 (12): 1619–1643.

Gettleman, Jeffrey. 2015. Meant to Keep Malaria Out, Mosquito Nets Are Used to Haul Fish In. *The New York Times*.

Grint, Keith. 2010. The Cuckoo Clock Syndrome: Addicted to Command, Allergic to Leadership. *European Management Journal* 28 (4) (August): 306–313.

Harmon, Michael M., and Richard T. Mayer. 1986. *Organization Theory for Public Administration*. Boston, MA: Little, Brown.

Head, Brian W. 2008. Wicked Problems in Public Policy. *Public Policy* 3 (2): 101–118.

Head, Brian W. 2010. How Can the Public Sector Resolve Complex Issues? Strategies for Steering, Administering and Coping. *Asia-Pacific Journal of Business Administration* 2 (1): 8–16.

Heifetz, Ronald A. 1994. *Leadership Without Easy Answers*. Cambridge, MA: The Belknap Press of Harvard University.

Heifetz, Ronald, Alexander Grashow, and Marty Linsky. 2009. *The Practice of Adaptive Leadership: Tools and Tactics for Changing Your Organization and the World*. Boston, MA: Harvard Business Press.

Innes, Judith E., and David Booher. 1999. Consensus Building and Complex Adaptive Systems. *Journal of the American Planning Association* 65 (4): 412–423.

Innes, Judith E., and David E. Booher. 2016. Collaborative Rationality as a Strategy for Working with Wicked Problems. *Landscape and Urban Planning* 154 (October): 8–10.

International Finance Corporation. 2019. Creating Impact: The Promise of Impact Investing, April. World Bank Group.

Kelly, Annie. 2019. Apple and Google Named in US Lawsuit over Congolese Child Cobalt Mining Deaths. *The Guardian*, December 16.

Kovacic, Samuel F., and Andres Sousa-Poza. 2013. *Managing and Engineering in Complex Situations*, vol. 21. Topics in Safety, Risk, Reliability and Quality. Dordrecht: Springer Netherlands.

Laub, Zachary. 2019. Hate Speech on Social Media: Global Comparisons, June 7. Council on Foreign Affairs.

Lawson, Max, Man-Kwun Chan, Francesca Rhodes, Anam Parvez Butt, Anna Marriott, Ellen Ehmke, Didier Jacobs, Julie Seghers, Jaime Atienza, and Rebecca Gowland. 2019. Public Good or Private Wealth, January. Oxfam.

Marshak, Robert J. 2008. Reflections on Wicked Problems in Organizations. *Journal of Management Inquiry* 18 (1) (August 12): 58–59.

MIT Technology Review. 2020. The Innovation Issue, July 2020.

Nicholls, Alex. 2012. The Legitimacy of Social Entrepreneurship: Reflexive Isomorphism in a Pre-Paradigmatic Field. *Social Enterprises: An Organizational Perspective* 44: 222–247.

Nicholls, Alex, Rob Paton, and Jed Emerson (eds.). 2015. *Social Finance*. Oxford, UK: Oxford University Press. https://doi.org/10.1093/acprof:oso/9780198703761.001.0001.

Pascale, Richard, Mark Milleman, and Linda Gioja. 2001. *Surfing the Edge of Chaos: The Laws of Nature and the New Laws of Business*, 229. New York: Crown Business.

Peterson, Gayle. 2010. *Wicked Problem Construct: Business and Social Sector Strategies for Global Change*. Saint Paul, MN: Headwaters Group.

Peterson, G., Yawson, R.M., Sherman, J., & Johnson Kanda, I. 2018. A systems model of using the Deliberate Leadership® framework for addressing wicked problems. *International Journal of Business and Systems Research* 12 (3): 262–289. https://doi.org/10.1504/IJBSR.2018.10010536.

Ponciano, Jonathan. 2019. The Largest Technology Companies in 2019: Apple Reigns as Smartphones Slip and Cloud Services Thrive. *Forbes Global 2000*.

Raworth, Kate. 2018. *Doughnut Economics: Seven Ways to Think Like a 21st-Century Economist*. London: Random House.

Rayner, Steve. 2006. Wicked Problems: Clumsy Solutions- Diagnoses and Prescriptions for Environmental Ills. In *Jack Beale Memorial Lecture on Global Environment*, 1–12. Sydney, NSW, Australia: James Martin Institute for Science and Civilization.

Rexhepi, Gadaf. 2017. The Architecture of Social Finance. In *Routledge Handbook of Social and Sustainable Finance*, ed. Othmar M. Lehner, 35–49. London, UK: Routledge.

Rigaud, Kanta Kumari, Alex de Sherbinin, Bryan Jones, Jonas Bergmann, Viviane Clement, Kayly Ober, Jacob Schewe, Susana Adamo, Brent McCusker, Silke Heuser, and Amelia Midgley. 2018. Groundswell: Preparing for Internal Climate Migration: 2. The World Bank.

Ritchey, Tom. 2011. *Wicked Problems—Social Messes*. Risk, Governance and Society. Berlin, Heidelberg: Springer Berlin Heidelberg.

Rittel, Horst W.J. 1972. On the Planning Crisis: Systems Analysis of the 'First and Second Generation'. *Bedriftskonomen* 8: 390–396.

Rittel, Horst W.J., and Melvin M. Webber. 1973. Dilemmas in a General Theory of Planning. *Policy Sciences* 4 (2) (June): 155–169.

Roberts, Nancy. 2000. The International Public Management Review IPMR: The e-Journal of the IPMN. *International Public Management Review* 1 (1): 1–19.

Schroders. 2019. Schroders Acquires Majority Stake in Leading Impact Investor Blue Orchard, July.

Schwab, Klaus. 2016. The Fourth Industrial Revolution: What It Means, How to Respond, January. World Economic Forum.

Senge, Peter M. 2006. *The Fifth Discipline: The Art & Practice of the Learning Organization*, Revised. New York, NY: Doubleday.

Sherman, John, and Gayle Peterson. 2009. Finding the Win in Wicked Problems: Lessons from Evaluating Public Policy Advocacy. *The Foundation Review* 1 (3) (October 1): 87–99.

Skaburskis, Andrejs. 2008. The Origin of 'Wicked Problems'. *Planning Theory and Practice* 9 (2): 277–280.

Stichler, Jaynelle F. 2009. Wicked Problems in Designing Healthcare Facilities. *The Journal of Nursing Administration* 39 (10): 405–408.

Stolterman, Erik. 2008. The Nature of Design Practice and Implications for Interaction Design Research. *International Journal of Design* 2 (1): 55–65.

Tetenbaum, Toby J. 1998. Shifting Paradigms: From Newton to Chaos. *Organizational Dynamics* 26 (4) (March): 21–32.

The Economist Intelligence Unit. 2018. Women and Millennials Reshaping Investing and Legacy in Asia. RBC Wealth Management.

The Global Impact Investing Network. 2018. Roadmap for the Future of Impact Investing: Reshaping Financial Markets, March. Global Impact Investing Network.

Townsend, Peter. 2016. *The Dark Side of Technology*. Oxford: Oxford University Press. ISBN 978-0-19-879053-2.

UBS Optimus Foundation. 2018. The Case for Social Finance. Supporting Innovation and Focusing on Results in Development. UBS Optimus Foundation.

United Nations Development Programme (UNDP). 1994. Human Development Report 1994: New Dimensions of Human Security. http://www.hdr.undp.org/en/content/human-development-report-1994.

United Nations Development Programme. 2017. Sustainable Development Goals. http://www.undp.org/content/undp/en/home/sustainable-development-goals.html.

Varga, Eva, and Malcolm Hayday. 2016. A Recipe Book for Social Finance: A Practical Guide on Designing and Implementing Initiatives to Develop Social Finance Instruments and Markets.

Weber, Axel A., and Sergio P. Ermotti. 2018. Partnerships for the Goals: Achieving the United Nations' Sustainable Development Goals, January. UBS.

World Bank. 2020. Updated Estimates of the Impact of COVID-19 on Global Poverty. https://blogs.worldbank.org/opendata/updated-estimates-impact-covid-19-global-poverty.

WEF. 2020. Global Risk Report 2020. World Economic Forum.

World Health Organization. 2018. World Malaria Report.

WWF. 2018. Coalition to End Wildlife Trafficking Online.

Yawson, Robert M. 2009. The Ecological System of Innovation: A New Architectural Framework for a Functional Evidence-based Platform for Science and Innovation Policy. In *The Future of Innovation. Proceedings of XX ISPIM 2009 Conference*, ed. K.R.E Huizingh, S. Conn, M. Torkkeli, and I. Bitran. Vienna, Austria: Wiley Higher Education.

Yawson, Robert M. 2015. The 'Wicked Problem Construct' for Organisational Leadership and Development. *International Journal of Business and Systems Research* 9 (1): 67–85.

CHAPTER 2

Wicked Problems and Deliberate Leadership: Finding True North

Deliberate Leadership Framework

This chapter discusses Deliberate Leadership as a strategy to help leaders across sectors address Wicked Problems. The term Deliberate Leadership comes from two sources. The first, a quote from poet and civil rights activist Audre Lorde who said, "I am deliberate and afraid of nothing." Leaders taking on Wicked Problems must be intentional and fearless. The term also comes from a colleague who a decade ago used the term in her Master's thesis to describe how individuals survive and thrive under extremely challenging circumstances. For her, it was surviving a childhood of poverty with alcoholic parents. She went on to be very successful in business, but recognized it was intentionality and fortitude that helped her overcome the challenges in life.

In this book, we use Deliberate Leadership—respecting the history of its origins—as an ethical framework for decision-making. Our research compared an amalgam of the most common leadership taught in business schools and taught worldwide to address complexity. What emerged were core values-based characteristics that are described in this chapter and illustrated through case examples throughout the book. Deliberate Leadership is built on collective thinking across disciplines and is the opposite of the autocratic leadership emerging today around the world. These characteristics, called the 7 C's by executive students to help them remember them, include:

G. Peterson et al., *Navigating Big Finance and Big Technology for Global Change*, Palgrave Studies in Impact Finance,
https://doi.org/10.1007/978-3-030-40712-4_2

- Courage to accept the challenge of taking on Wicked Problems and working within a complex system.
- Collaboration to draw upon divergent voices within and beyond the walls of an organization.
- Creativity to imagine different scenarios for the future.
- Community to put those who are at the center of social change at the table.
- Candor to speak the truth about what is and isn't working.
- Capital to value social, environmental, and financial assets.
- Compassion to make decisions based on empathy.

There are other relevant C's that have surfaced in our research. Context and communications are important. Social investors must consider political, social, and environmental context of place in which investment decisions are to be made. Communications is also critically important to openly describe and share learning and experiences to enable the field of social finance to benefit.

The Deliberate Leadership framework is relevant at individual, organizational, and societal levels. In this chapter, academic Robert Yawson, substantiates the theory behind the seven dimensions of Deliberate Leadership. Subsequent chapters illustrate how that theory is used in practice. The approach is applied within and beyond the walls of an organization. As illustrated in Fig. 2.1, values and beliefs shape the organizational

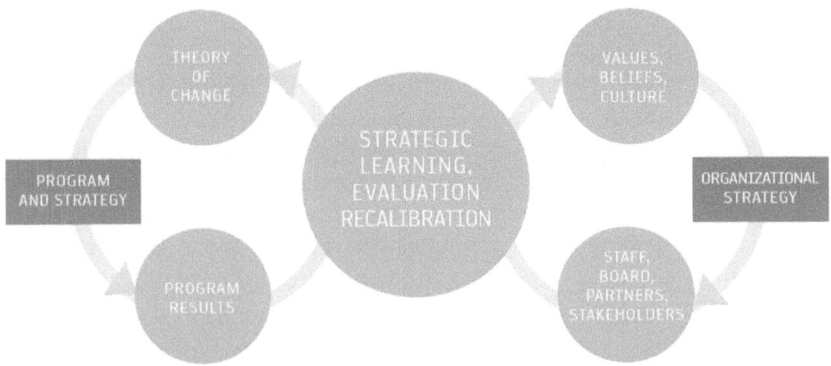

Fig. 2.1 Leadership and organizational culture in supporting innovation (*Source* Reproduced with permission from pfc social impact advisors llc.)

culture which in turn shapes the theory of change for an investment strategy and the programmatic outcomes. It shapes how an organization learns, adapts, and grows to address complex challenges.

Courage

Deliberate Leadership requires *Courage* to acknowledge risk and ambiguity, and to diagnose the leadership approach appropriate for addressing Wicked Problems. Organizations are situated within morally complex internal and external environments, requiring leaders to possess levels of moral courage sufficient to promote ethical action, while refraining from unethical actions when faced with temptations or pressures (Hannah et al. 2011). There is no single definition of leader courage in the management literature. However, the general theme across the various definitions include: A state of character, a quality of mind, a character virtue, an attitude, a construction, a competency, or an act (Harbour and Kisfalvi 2014).

The importance of leaders and followers speaking out if they encounter wrongdoing, but also recognizing the serious obstacles and negative consequences that they may face in doing so (as well as the need for organizational and institutional processes and structures to facilitate such action), is at the heart of Deliberate Leadership (Harbour and Kisfalvi 2014). Courageous leaders must be equipped with both practical and theoretical understandings of concepts such as chaos and complexity theory, and complex adaptive practice using an ecosystem change model. Given the intractable Wicked Problems facing twenty-first-century organizations and requiring difficult leadership decisions, there is no better time for a richer understanding of the qualities underlying the choice to act with courage (Amos and Klimoski 2014). Deliberate Leaders recognize that moral action is inherently risky but continue to model ethical behavior despite the apparent danger. They refuse to excuse their values to go along with the group, to keep silent when customers may be hurt, or to lie to investors and other stakeholders (Johnson 2015). "They continue to carry out the organization's mission even in the face of dangers and uncertainty" (Johnson 2015).

The courage to take risks is reflected in the extent to which leaders and organizations unflinchingly explore a range of options to address a problem, assess the threats and opportunities of those different options (i.e., scenario planning), and then act. Organizations may claim to be risk-takers, however when confronted with a problem, they jump to a solution in a framework with which they are familiar. Jeffrey Conklin calls this the "Answer Reflex" (Conklin 2006). They also feel more comfortable following structure when approaching problems.

Deliberate Leaders have the courage to analyze and understand their blind spots and embrace that they do not know the answers. Scenario planning challenges organizations to test their mental models and to allow multiple perspectives to be heard, to accelerate collaborative learning, and to align vision and solutions (Shearer 2004). It can be linked, for instance, to threat-opportunity analysis (see Fig. 2.2) to better understand unanticipated opportunities and threats, and to be prepared to adapt when such opportunities and threats arise (as they undoubtedly will).

Scenario planning is especially appropriate given the uncertainty and dynamic complexity of Wicked Problems. Faced with an uncertain landscape, strategic planning is difficult. Deliberate Leaders need a framework that allows them to maneuver in an uncertain environment and to make decisions that can prepare them for dealing with future Wicked Problems (Yawson 2013). "In a highly uncertain environment, the advantages of scenario planning are clear: since no one base case can be regarded as probable, it's necessary to develop plans on the assumption that several

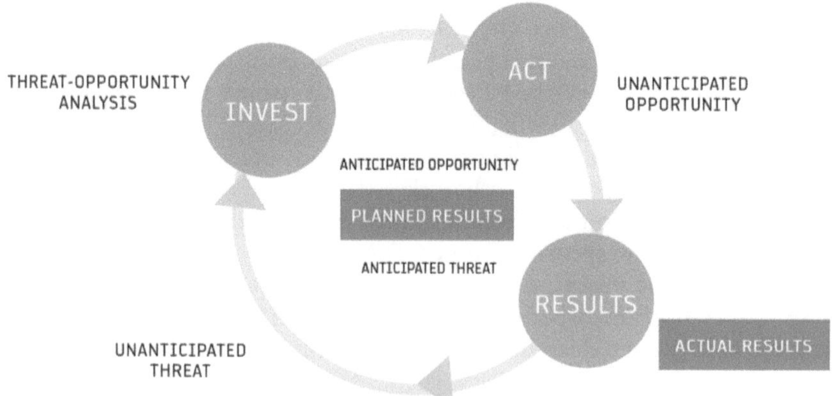

Fig. 2.2 Deliberate Leadership threats and opportunities analysis (*Source* Reproduced with permission from pfc social impact advisors llc.)

different futures are possible" (Ramírez and Selin 2014). As scenarios accept structural uncertainty with multiple interpretations and multiple futures, they present opportunities for Deliberate Leaders to identify multiple alternatives in addressing Wicked Problems (Ramirez et al. 2015).

Collaboration

Deliberate Leadership requires *Collaboration* to reach out to individuals and organizations with diverse perspectives on problem-solving can lead to the greatest innovation. "Differences in convictions, cultural values, and operating norms inevitably add complexity to collaborative efforts. But they also make them richer, more innovative, and more valuable. Getting that value is the heart of collaborative leadership" (Ibarra and Hansen 2011). These diverse voices can include business, arts, social services, social media and journalism, and internal collaboration across teams and departments in addition to external partnerships. Tools used to build internal collaborations include creating boundary-less organizations as well as external partnerships. Effective relationships break down silos and share knowledge more easily. "Leaders today must be able to harness ideas, people, and resources from across boundaries of all kinds" (Ibarra and Hansen 2011).

Catalytic alliances have been used effectively to build diverse collaborations. First described by Waddock and Post (1995), catalytic alliances operate at the leading edge of social reform by leveraging resources by mobilizing others to act. Alliances work through a robust network of organizations to address a social issue. Unlike other forms of collaboration, catalytic alliances avoid direct intervention, preferring instead to work through public and private efforts to effectively address a problem. In catalytic alliances, risk is shared among collaborators and therefore minimizing risks for individual partners. These collaborations are vision-driven and address "non-zero sum" problems where one stakeholder's success does not come at the expense of another actor; both can win or lose.

There are many examples of collaboration in the Wicked Problem context. NEON, the New Economy Organisers Network, for example, builds the strength of movements for social and economic justice, influencing how the British public understands the economy. It does this by creating compelling messages and generating a mass of voices from across civil society demanding a shift to an economic system that meets people's real needs within ecological boundaries. Sistema B is a Latin American movement of banks and other businesses collaborating to balance purpose and profit, and to use business as a force for good. The movement supports the creation of B Corporations, private companies that generate public goods and profits for shareholders. Conventional companies—ones focused on the financial bottom line alone—enjoy networks and alliances of diverse actors that help them thrive. Management consultants, financial institutions, academics, and legal advisors are just a few of the actors conventional companies can draw on. Sistema B seeks to create something similar attuned to the needs of B Corps. It works through building alliances with other players, promoting communities of practice that achieve synergies across diverse players, and the creation of dedicated actors, new Sistema Bs, at local and national levels in Argentina, Colombia, and Brazil.

NEON and Sistema B are examples of different types of collaboration. Deliberate Leadership doesn't define any single type that has to be used to address Wicked Problems. For example, Kania and Kramer (2011) identify five types of collaborations, any of which might be appropriate depending on the circumstances:

1. Funder collaborations: A group of funders interested in the same issue pooling their resources.
2. Public–private partnerships: Partnerships between private and government organizations.
3. Multi-stakeholder initiatives: Voluntary effort from various stakeholders around a common theme.
4. Social sector networks: Ad hoc groupings of individuals and organizations with an emphasis on information sharing and short-term solutions.
5. Collective impact initiatives: Long-term groupings of actors from various sectors sharing a common agenda for solving a specific societal problem.

Deliberate Leadership requires the humility to recognize that no one person has the answers and that partners have to share the responsibility of finding "clumsy" (imperfect) solutions, while accepting that it may well take a long time, with some trial and error. Deliberate Leadership is about the art of humble inquiry, democratizing work, and listening to all the relevant voices.

Creativity

Deliberate Leadership requires *Creativity* to imagine a new future and to develop "Big Ideas" through scenario planning or other approaches that help create unique social change solutions. Deliberate Leaders acknowledge that in a complex world of Wicked Problems, there is no one-size-fits-all solution. Being creative means that one does not rely on any fixed way of doing things (Zhang 2014).

Social innovation is one form of creativity that is relevant to social finance. Socially innovative actions, strategies, practices, and processes occur in response to Wicked Problems (Moulaert et al. 2007). Social innovation is necessary because, as already highlighted, linear thinking does not help us deal with wicked, complex, intractable challenges. No single actor, private or public, has the authority or capability to address conditions such as poverty, exclusion, segregation, and deprivation in ways that they manifest themselves today (Moulaert et al. 2007).

Nicholls et al. (2015) describe social innovation as: "Varying levels of deliberative novelty that bring about change and that aim to address suboptimal issues in the production, availability, and consumption of public goods defined as that which is broadly of societal benefit within a particular normative and culturally contingent context." Social innovation also occurs when faced with the adaptive challenge of opportunities for improving living conditions, like meeting the Sustainable Development Goals (SDGs). However, social innovation does not occur in a vacuum. It requires Deliberate Leadership values and norms. Addressing Wicked Problems through business practices and social innovations requires Deliberate Leadership and organizational development strategies for helping organizations mirror practices and approaches internally with staff and externally with stakeholders (Peterson et al. 2018). Mainemelis et al. (2015) have described creative leadership as leading others toward the attainment of creative outcomes, which entails three alternative manifestations: facilitating employee creativity; directing the materialization of a leader's creative vision; and integrating heterogeneous creative contributions.

The role of creativity as part of organizational culture and its effect on an organization's effectiveness and competitiveness have been widely studied. There are various definitions of organizational culture; however, organizational culture generally refers to the values and beliefs communicated through organizational norms, artifacts, and observed in behavioral patterns (Hogan and Coote 2014). Deliberate Leadership values guide behaviors and set a broad framework for organizational routines and practices (Hatch 1993). By emphasizing and exhibiting certain values, and by building corresponding norms for expected behaviors, leaders create an organizational culture and an enabling organizational climate that have a powerful and compelling influence on employee behavior and creativity, spurring the innovation process (Mumford et al. 2002). These values and norms can in turn manifest in artifacts (e.g., organizational rituals, language and stories, and physical configurations) and lead to desired outcomes such as innovation (Hogan and Coote 2014).

Just as innovation propelled the growth of impact investing more than a decade ago, various financial innovations are occurring to mobilize capital on the scale needed to stimulate markets for social purposes. Every innovation is, however, a two-edged sword, and social finance innovation is no different. It is important that organizations in the leading edge of social finance innovation have the organizational infrastructure that underpins programmatic strategy, which in turn decides theories of change and program results. This requires that leadership values and organizational norms act as a filter for how organizations perceive the external environment and shape strategic choice, behavior, and ultimately organizational performance.

Community

Deliberate Leadership requires *Community* to invest with and in local, place-based solutions such as those offered by positive deviance and tempered radicalism. The Wicked Problems that twenty-first-century organizations face necessitate new ways of organizing human collective activity and therefore the need for Deliberate Leadership. Doing things "smart" and "right" based on community feedback is a fundamental tenet of Deliberate Leadership. It starts immediately with mapping out partners and stakeholders in an ecosystem, putting community at the center, and identifying who is working in the interconnected ecosystem.

Communities of practice should not be a picture of people with shared values and beliefs working harmoniously, in joint endeavor, with unity of purpose; they should rather involve a more robust engagement with the hard realities (not just the clichés) of practices like inclusivity, collaboration, and diversity (Kirk and Shutte 2004). The community dimension of Deliberate Leadership emerges through a process of dialogue, connectivity, and empowerment within communities of different people who come together in collaborative endeavor (Kirk and Shutte 2004).

Figure 2.3 supports the thought exercise of assessing the ecosystem of stakeholders during the planning phase of deciding how to take on a Wicked Problem. It is designed to help leaders understand who else is working on similar issues, and to see potential allies and political or economic challenges that might get in the way. It is not intended to open up the process to everyone in the constellation, but to help understand the landscape in which their work occurs. Figure 2.3 illustrates how to map organizations within the ecosystems working to address human security in part of Africa and the range of possible partners—corporations, international NGOs, multilateral agencies, Africa-based funders,

Fig. 2.3 Deliberate Leader ecosystem of organizations working on human security (*Source* Reproduced with permission from pfc social impact advisors llc. 2016. ClimateWorks Foundation: Lessons in Leadership and Learning)

and international foundations. The photograph of a local woman and child at the center is a reminder of those most impacted by human security issues, and the potential organizations across disciplines that might be unusual advocates and allies.

The development of the landscape maps is situated in systems, complexity, and stakeholder theories (Yawson and Greiman 2014). In developing the maps, we use the dimensions of the UN Human Security Frame as our unit of analysis. Using the Dimensions of Human Security—community, economic, educational, environmental, food, health, personal, and political, we describe holistically the Human Security dimensions in the particular landscape to understand the universe in which the specific funder operates and the intersections that exist (Yawson et al. 2020). Building a holistic view is important because increases in security at one dimension do not replace nor eliminate demands at other dimensions. On the contrary, insecurity at one of the eight dimensions affects the other dimensions. Understanding human security as greater than the sum of its parts implies better coordination of the different dimensions, and help in developing more sustainable funding and policies to address the Wicked Problems at the intersection of the various dimensions.

Deliberate Leaders realize that every landscape is already populated by interested parties and that to be effective they must understand this population and build relationships among them. They also remember that community-based stakeholders can strengthen solutions to Wicked Problems such as climate change. By building partnerships of respect and collaboration with local voices, philanthropy, for instance, gains the insights needed to respond effectively to Wicked Problems and minimize the unintended consequences that sometimes result from interventions.

Leaders need to amplify the voices of the powerless, and listen to people who are not power brokers but who are "positive deviants" (Heifetz 1994; Pascale et al. 2010). Those are the people within every organization, community, and society who do things a little differently, innovate quietly, and discover unexpected solutions. Their suggestions and strategies can drive the response to a Wicked Problem in unexpected, more creative, and more successful directions.

Candor

Deliberate Leadership requires *Candor* to facilitate constant learning, reflection, and recalibration. These tools call for double-loop learning to deepen strategic learning by reexamining strategy, values, beliefs, and alignment framework: to understand intention and experience for organizations to practice espoused values. Bolton (2008) defines candor as an "interpersonal process that promotes the authentic expression of different points of view in search of actionable wisdom."

Deliberate Leaders create an organizational environment where every member is able to speak candidly. A prerequisite for candor is authenticity. It is the leader's job to create systems and norms that lead to a culture of candor. Meeting the expectations of others, Deliberate Leadership is about challenging the status quo, discussing the topics considered taboo, and naming the elephants in the room (Heifetz et al. 2009). (The threats-opportunity analysis discussed in the section on courage offers one opportunity for leaders to demonstrate candor.)

Ensuring ongoing alignment and adjustments of intentions, expectations, and outcomes requires candid conversations among stakeholders. Moingeon and Lefranc (2004) posit that alignment begins with the ways in which an organization internally identifies the intended customer experience; how it ensures that the offered experience aligns with the intended one; and how the expected experience offered to the customer aligns with the experience the customer actually lives. At the conceptual level, management sees the intended experience made manifest for the customer in an "expected experience." In reality, the conceptual or strategic notion is made operational when the organization "offers" an experience that is "lived" by the customer. Figure 2.4 illustrates these relationships.

Lack of alignment between intended and offered, offered and lived, or expected and lived experiences reduces an organization's effectiveness and, consequently, its ability to address the Wicked Problem. The inability of leadership to be candid about its conceptual expectations and how those are communicated, and to seek candor from the other stakeholders about how they are perceiving and living those expectations, allows misalignment to continue until a crisis is reached (as manifested in loss of funder support and reduced effectiveness of the funder).

The need to keep an organization focused and, at the same time, allow it to be creative and flexible in order to deal with Wicked Problems that arise is a challenge. It becomes even more challenging when

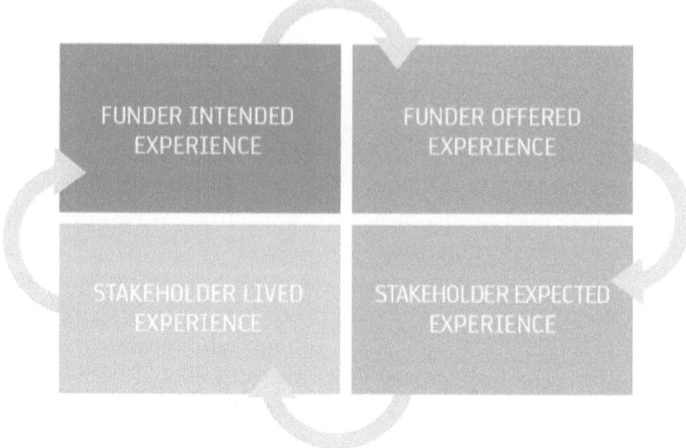

Fig. 2.4 Deliberate Leader alignment framework (*Source* Reproduced with permission from pfc social impact advisors llc.)

the expectations of alignment are within and across a network of organizations, and yet, as already noted, collaboration between organizations and recognizing the interrelationship of multiple stakeholders are essential for tackling Wicked Problems effectively. A well-developed alignment framework allows an organization or group to clearly articulate what is important and then to allow this to be the main driver of all activities performed throughout the organization or the network of organizations. Individual organizations should be both aligned to the strategy and to the needs of other partners in the network.

The nature of partnerships required to build a social finance ecosystem increases the complexity of management processes, in that each partner seeks to maximize the returns to the goals of their own organization as well as achieving the aims of the partnership. It requires a Deliberate Leadership approach to manage the complexities associated with these partnerships. By building on the resource complementarities of the partners, the intended outcome is that all players in the ecosystem gain from the partnership (Doherty et al. 2014). True partnership is about identifying shared value and leveraging the combined strengths of each partner to achieve a level of impact that could not be accomplished independently. This type of partnership is broadly referred to as Social Sector Partnerships.

While there is no ambiguity about the value of partnerships, unlocking their full potential means moving the conversation from "why partner" to "how to partner" (KPMG 2016). Organizations that are eager to engage in partnership oftentimes overlook some key questions amidst the enthusiasm of working together. Partnerships can be very fragile and may run the risk of internal tensions and mission drift due to holding incompatible goals, which makes it difficult to achieve financial sustainability and social impact. Identifying how leaders in such partnerships are able to address these challenges—through design structures, governance mechanisms, and performance management systems—is important to the understanding of how organizations can better align the generation of profit and achieve societal impact (Santos et al. 2015). Deliberate Leaders seek to establish and maintain alignment among their partners and collaborators, including the communities in which they work and serve, through open communication and candid conversations. Misalignment of purpose and values can cause inefficiencies in execution and less than optimal results and at worst, upend the collective effort completely.

Using funder–stakeholder communications as an illustrative example, Fig. 2.4 indicates the four places where such misalignments can occur—what is intended to be communicated among partners, what is actually communicated (i.e., what is the offered experience), the partners' expectations created by such communications (i.e., the experience they were offered), and how partners act on those communications or perceived agreements (Moingeon and Lefranc 2004).

The relationship between social investor and partners in a social finance initiative offers many opportunities for misalignment. The social investor naturally intends to meet a need or respond to a problem successfully and make social and financial returns on investment, and also intends to be responsive to and respectful of the needs and expectations of its partners. The partners—service providers, outcome funders, etc., have expectations as well, and those may not perfectly align with the intentions of the investor. Finally, what the partner experiences may not be what they expected.

Every partnership is unique, but there is a broad similarity in how organizations engage with each other and develop a partnership. At every stage in the partnership process there are rewards and challenges, and candor to facilitate constant learning, reflection, and recalibration at every stage is critical.

Capital

Deliberate Leadership requires *Capital* to invest in sustainable long-term solutions and to recognize the value of multiple bottom lines: social, environmental, and financial objectives. Deliberate Leaders believe that taking care of profits, people, and the planet is critical to organizational success, both now and in the future. The capital dimension of Deliberate Leadership includes financial, social, and environmental capital.

Social capital theories address relationships among people and institutions and the development of trust between people (Williams and Durrance 2008). Deliberate Leaders steer their organizations to play a significant role in the development of civil society because they offer a means by which people can work collaboratively toward shared goals of community improvement. Through this, leaders and their organizations develop social capital, a valuable accumulation of knowledge, experience, and trust that can then be tapped to support ongoing efforts to improve the community (Seibert et al. 2001).

The blended pursuit of social and financial return on investment is an effective approach for long-term sustainability. Nonprofit organizations can benefit from the triple bottom line of people, planet, profit, particularly when competing for funds and funding partners. They can also partner with for-profit organizations and experience greater social impact as well as increased financial stability. When nonprofit organizations diversify their revenue stream, report the triple bottom line, and focus on long-term organizational goals, they are better equipped to meet the challenges inherent in pursuing positive social impact (Milde and Yawson 2017). In the case of social finance, the central theme of this book, there are the added challenges of moving the needle on the "investing" side as it requires mainstream finance to no longer view social finance instruments as concessionary products. The value of multiple bottom lines will continue to grow in importance as consumers, members, and donors remain adamant in their demand for proof of social impact and fiscal responsibility.

As nonprofit organizations respond to the increased public demand for accountability, they can further enhance the triple bottom line by fully embracing the opportunities available through technology. Social media,

Artificial Intelligence, Internet of Things, and Blockchain provide new options that can help organizations meet the triple bottom line. These technologies represent the next frontier for nonprofit and hybrid organizations. Social media allows an expanded base of stewards to connect and engage with each other. Artificial Intelligence and blockchain technology offer a completely new way for organizations to obtain funding, as well as affordable, scalable avenues to increase transparency and traceability in the supply chain, allowing workers to provide anonymous, real-time feedback directly to corporate leadership. Thoughtful integration of the organization's mission with the technological tools available can further enhance an organization's ability to affect change while meeting the triple bottom line (Milde and Yawson 2017). As we discuss in more detail in Chapter 5, Deliberate Leadership recognizes that organizations are well served when they effectively use technology to achieve social, environmental, and financial change.

Compassion

Deliberate Leadership requires *Compassion* to drive solutions through empathy rather than ego or command-and-control techniques. There is a deep need for compassionate organizations where employees feel empowered and encouraged to tackle the Wicked Problems and adaptive challenges of the twenty-first century (Kanov et al. 2004).

Compassion and related concepts such as concern, care, empathy, kindness, generosity, and love all refer to an orientation that puts others ahead of the self (Peterson and Seligman 2004). Theorists from different disciplines have diverse view on compassion. The concept of compassion dates back more than 2000 years and is studied within such diverse fields as philosophy, psychology, religion, management, human resource development, and sociology (Bejou 2011). A compassionate leader has a powerful impact and a motivating effect on followers to work together and to make sacrifices of their own. Deliberate Leadership recognizes that compassion flows when individual intentions are aligned with organizational value systems, along with the provision of resources (Banker and Bhal 2018). Compassion as a Deliberate Leadership attribute creates a stronger sense of group identity and enables employees to perform better on tasks while avoiding the dangers of groupthink.

Deliberate Leadership promotes compassion within organizations by incorporating compassion into their vision, mission, goals, values, culture, decisions, strategy, and operations to have a positive and measurable footprint on the communities they serve while addressing the challenges of Wicked Problems facing global society. Bejou (2011) identified 10 core values of compassionate organizations:

1. Adherence to the principles of integrity.
2. Action in support of human rights and welfare (shareholders, employees, customers, women, children).
3. Action against global social ills (poverty, disease, disaster, others).
4. Action in support of family and community needs (roads, schools, hospitals, others).
5. Support for freedom.
6. Responsible workplace practices.
7. Support for animal rights and welfare.
8. Action in support of environmental sustainability.
9. Excellence in corporate shared governance.
10. Excellence in corporate and social performance.

One important element in the brave new world of social finance is the creation of partnerships and catalytic alliances. However, conflicting priorities can create emotional distress and cognitive dissonance, resulting in reduced compassion among partners (Zulueta 2015). "Human interaction and subjectivity make organizational compassion a complex process that may raise concerns, especially regarding the extent to which compassion can affect the organization in other areas" (Shahzad and Muller 2016). Deliberate Leadership is cognizant of this potential barrier to developing compassionate alliances. The ability to inculcate the 7 C's is a way of preventing this from occurring.

Deliberate Leader Learning Process

The seven characteristics of Deliberate Leadership apply equally across all three phases of the process by which organizations learn and adapt in order to deal successfully with Wicked Problems. Organizational learning is important at both the programmatic and operational levels; the learning process must apply in both. The three phases of organizational learning and change are: Phase I: "Partner and Plan," to establish the methods to achieve the investor's financial return and the impact on the community;

Phase II: "Act and Assess," to help the investor implement their portfolio investment strategies; and Phase III: "Reflect and Recalibrate" provides a mechanism to assess whether the investor has achieved their desired financial and nonfinancial returns, and if not to have the foresight to make the necessary adjustments going forward (Fig. 2.5).

Each phase is tied to the others, and learning and recalibration are circular and occur with both partners externally and colleagues internally. Alignment in both program and operations is needed to ensure continuous and robust impact and learning

Deliberate Leaders know when they take on a Wicked Problem they will fail and learn, recover, and improve. But when a program has been sold as a solution to board members, investors, colleagues, and partners, it is hard to admit things may not be working out as planned. A Deliberate Leader understands that failures come early, and success takes time. Leaders must be prepared for both successes and failures, seeing both as an opportunity to learn. Early failures generate systemic learning about where opportunities are (and are not) and how to address them. A low failure rate may not signify success—on the contrary, it may mean the

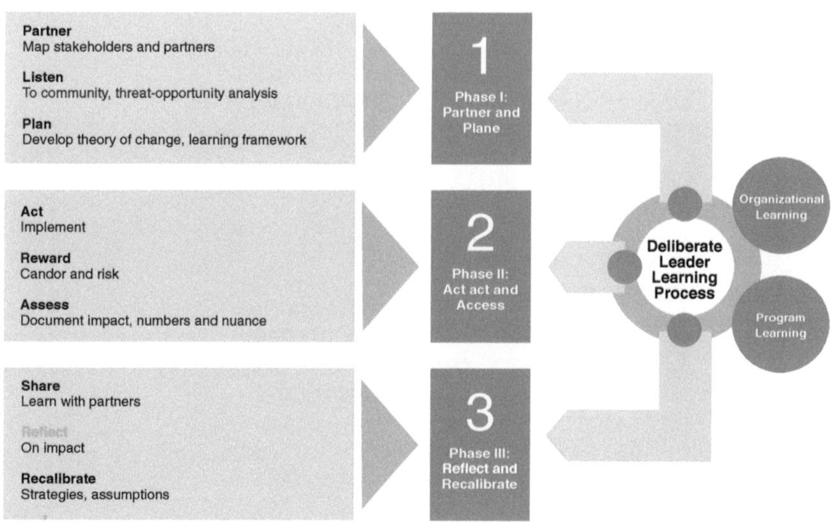

Fig. 2.5 Deliberate Leader learning process (*Source* Reproduced with permission from pfc social impact advisors llc.)

organization lacked courage in tackling a Wicked Problem, or it may mean the organization does not protect truth-telling and reward honesty.

Furthermore, learning is not just a matter of getting better at doing what you are already doing. Deep learning requires fundamental reflection on the way you work and at times making fundamental changes in your modes of operating. This is the process of reflection and recalibration, graphically depicted in Fig. 2.6.

While the Deliberate Leadership analytic construct sees data gathering and assessment as part of each stage of activity—in Phase I, to identify partners and stakeholders and properly define the problem being addressed; in Phase II, for ongoing assessment in parallel with action—a particular, deeper kind of learning occurs in Phase III. Double-loop learning (Argyris 1977) helps leaders and their organizations make informed decisions in rapidly changing and uncertain times. This deeper and more adaptive form of assessment rests on several principles: commitment to robust learning, testing hypotheses, openly sharing results, and recognizing that program outcomes are shaped by values, beliefs,

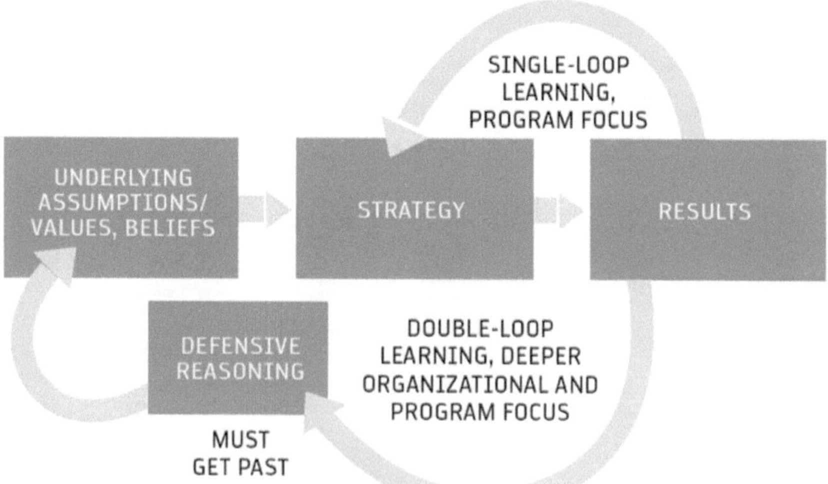

Fig. 2.6 Deliberate Leader reflection and recalibration (*Source* Reproduced with permission from pfc social impact advisors llc.)

and assumptions as well as by strategy. It involves profound life-cycle examination and learning (Bolman and Deal 2008).

The kind of learning that typically occurs in Phases I and II—Did we find the right partners? Are we doing what we set out to do? Are we getting results?—does not address Wicked Problems because it involves single-loop learning (Yawson 2015). Wicked problems have no room for single-loop learning. The Deliberate Leader understands and knows how to get past defensive and rational reasoning to test the underlying assumptions, values and beliefs, and to recalibrate. This is how Wicked Problems are addressed in these complex and challenging times.

Senge et al. (2010) in their book *The Necessary Revolution: Working Together to Create a Sustainable World* characterized times of such complexity and challenge as providing the context for growing the capacity for everyone to shape the future they desire, individually and collectively. This capacity-building requires unlearning old assumptions and biases that obstruct the discovery of shared purpose and learning the means to enact new collective visions. Senge et al. (2010) make the case for double-loop learning (or changes in underlying frameworks) that helps in learning how to examine the assumptions and mental models governing our actions. As they put it, there is a need for "the necessary revolution," and contend that the people leading this revolution demonstrate mastery of three core areas that undergird organizational learning: learning how to see the larger systems; understanding the importance of collaborating across boundaries "that previously divided them from others within and outside their organizations," and "moving away from reactive problem solving mode to creating futures they truly desire" (Yawson 2015).

Learning that is procreative involves mutual engagement with new possibilities, and results in expanded creativity, deeper participation, and self- and/or collective transformation, as is being seen in social finance and impact investing. Procreative learning enables task completion within shorter periods of time, while also building capacity for longer-term complex thinking and expanding kinds of reasoning, particularly the inductive and abductive reasoning needed for complexity and chaotic learning (Nicolaides and Marsick 2016).

Deliberate Leadership solicits feedback from internal and external communities. Internal communities include everyone from leaders to frontline staff within an organization. External communities include the beneficiaries of an organization's actions and programs, and the peer anchors feedback in systems and complexity theories. These theories maintain that relationships in complex systems, like organizations, are nonlinear, made up of interconnections and branching choices that produce unintended consequences and render the universe unpredictable. Complexity theory posits that some events, given our knowledge and technology, are unknowable until they occur, and may indeed be unknowable in advance (Yawson 2013). In this context, a "feedback mechanism" is an information system that can determine whether the outputs of a system are what they ought to be, and can be used to adjust inputs and processes in order to improve outputs and ensure that they are closer to intended goals.

It is easy to confuse "input" information collected to design new programs and theories of change, with "feedback" (Threlfall 2013). Feedback can only be said to exist between two parts or groups when they interact with and affect each other (Threlfall 2013). Ideally, feedback mechanisms ought to create systems that are self-regulating. This can be achieved through double-loop learning—i.e., not merely adjusting strategy implementation based on feedback results, but instituting processes that overcome defensive reasoning to question and criticize underlying organizational and programmatic assumptions, values, and beliefs. An organization may have reasons to mistakenly believe that it already has robust feedback loops in place. Monitoring and evaluation activities, ad hoc site visits, and outcomes measurement workshops can often look and feel like listening and learning from feedback. The key difference is that, while monitoring and evaluation are assessments based on the priorities of funders, managers, and independent experts, feedback prioritizes the voices of stakeholders who lack formal authority, like community members and junior staff.

A more insidious concern is that even when organizations set up feedback loops that are separate from monitoring and evaluation efforts, these loops are often faulty. This may be due to a lack of tools or knowledge to solicit feedback in a routine manner that is "reliable, rigorous and useful" (Twersky et al. 2013). Site visits may not be a systematic method of collecting data, surveys may be of poor quality, information may be difficult to interpret without benchmarks and, most commonly, organizations may not have completed the crucial step of closing the loop by acting on and sharing the feedback they collect (Twersky et al. 2013).

Conclusion

This book is not intended to be prescriptive and provide definitive answers to address complex issues. Rather, it is designed to stimulate thinking chapter. In this chapter we have done this by pinpointing the Deliberate Leadership characteristics needed to address the world's most complex challenges, offering insight to leaders as they use new forms of blended capital to tackle the Wicked Problems of the twenty-first century.

A commitment to using Deliberate Leadership requires leaders to create, nurture, and continually reinforce an organizational culture dedicated to open and honest learning, adaptation, communication, and diverse stakeholder involvement. It also requires organizations to let go of the need to have only the "right" answers, of focusing on short-term outcomes and impacts, and controlling the process unilaterally. These commitments often mean a substantial change in institutional culture. Organizations trying to establish new norms include the American Sustainable Business Institute (ASBI), a network of businesses and business associations working together for policies and practices that generate broad prosperity, environmental protection and regeneration, and human well-being. ASBI seeks to leverage the voice and power of the business community to advance an economy that recognizes Wicked Problems, one based on renewable energy, clean water, safer chemicals, regenerative agriculture, and high road business practices. Another example where institutional culture is being changed through an emphasis on the qualities of Deliberate Leadership is the B Lab's work to extend principles of the 'B Economy' to multinational corporations. Stressing characteristics such as collaboration, creativity and community, it aims to engage multinationals in collective action to advance stakeholder governance and to amplify strategic planning around urgent collective action associated with Wicked Problems. That action involves measurable impact and legal accountability, but also culture change to improve multinational business practices, promote stakeholder governance, and influence investors and policymakers.

These are just two examples of organizations breaking the mold and trying to establish a new normal. The array of organizations in this kind of social innovation is diverse, and when efforts are driven by the efforts of multiple stakeholders using the principles of Deliberate Leadership, they stimulate new forms of creativity that are quite different from the linear problem solving of the past. Addressing Wicked Problems requires a significant cultural shift for many organizations, whether they are corporations, funders, grantees, or other stakeholders.

References

Amos, Benjamin, and Richard J. Klimoski. 2014. Courage: Making Teamwork Work Well. *Group and Organization Management* 39 (1): 110–128.

Argyris, Chris. 1977. Double Loop Learning in Organizations. *Harvard Business Review* 55 (5): 115–125.

Banker, Darshna V., and Kanika T. Bhal. 2018. Understanding Compassion from Practicing Managers' Perspective: Vicious and Virtuous Forces in Business Organizations. *Global Business Review* 20 (6) (February 19): 1–17.

Bejou, David. 2011. Compassion as the New Philosophy of Business. *Journal of Relationship Marketing* 10 (1): 1–6.

Bolman, Lee G., and Terrence E. Deal. 2008. *Reframing Organizations: Artistry, Choice, and Leadership*, 4th ed. San Francisco, CA: Jossey-Bass.

Bolton, James. 2008. The Candor Imperative. *IEEE Engineering Management Review* 36 (1): 157.

Conklin, Jeff. 2006. Wicked Problems and Social Complexity. In *Dialogue Mapping: Building Understanding of Wicked Problems*, ed. Jeff Conklin. Hoboken, NJ: Wiley.

Doherty, Bob, Helen Haugh, and Fergus Lyon. 2014. Social Enterprises as Hybrid Organizations: A Review and Research Agenda. *International Journal of Management Reviews* 16 (4): 417–436. https://doi.org/10.1111/ijmr.12028.

Hannah, Sean T., Bruce J. Avolio, and Fred O. Walumbwa. 2011. Relationships Between Authentic Leadership, Moral Courage, and Ethical Pro-Social Behaviors. *Business Ethics Quarterly* 21 (4): 555–578.

Harbour, Michelle, and Veronika Kisfalvi. 2014. In the Eye of the Beholder: An Exploration of Managerial Courage. *Journal of Business Ethics* 119 (4): 493–515.

Hatch, Mary J.O. 1993. The Dynamics of Organizational Culture. *Academy of Management Review* 18 (4): 657–693.

Heifetz, Ronald A. 1994. *Leadership Without Easy Answers*. Cambridge, MA: The Belknap Press of Harvard University.

Heifetz, Ronald A., Alexander Grashow, and Marty Linsky. 2009. *The Practice of Adaptive Leadership: Tools and Tactics for Changing Your Organization and the World*. Boston, MA: Harvard Business Press.

Hogan, Suellen J., and Leonard V. Coote. 2014. Organizational Culture, Innovation, and Performance: A Test of Schein's Model. *Journal of Business Research* 67 (8): 1609–1621.

Ibarra, Herminia, and Morten T. Hansen. 2011. Are You a Collaborative Leader? *Harvard Business Review* 89 (July–August): 68–74.

Johnson, Craig E. 2015. *Meeting the Ethical Challenges of Leadership—Casting Light or Shadow*, 5th ed. Thousand Oaks, CA: Sage.

Kania, John, and Mark Kramer. 2011. Collective Impact. *Stanford Social Innovation Review* 9 (1): 36–41.

Kanov, Jason M., Sally Maitlis, Monica C. Worline, Jane E. Dutton, Peter J. Frost, and Jacoba M. Lilius. 2004. Compassion in Organizational Life. *American Behavioral Scientist* 47 (6): 808–827.

Kirk, Philip, and Anna Marie Shutte. 2004. Community Leadership Development. *Community Development Journal* 39 (3): 234–251.

KPMG International. 2016. *Unlocking the Power of Partnership—A Framework for Effective Cross-Sector Collaboration to Advance the Global Goals for Sustainable Development. 528878.* Washington, DC: International Development Services, KPMG International.

Mainemelis, Charalampos, Ronit Kark, and Olga Epitropaki. 2015. Creative Leadership: A Multi-Context Conceptualization. *The Academy of Management Annals* 9 (1) (May): 1–122.

Milde, Katherine, and Robert M. Yawson. 2017. Strategies for Social Media Use in Nonprofits. *Journal of Management Policy and Practice* 18 (1): 19–27.

Moingeon, Bertrand, and Elisabeth LeFranc. 2004. Overcoming Obstacles to Innovation. *PCM Bridge* 102 (10): 31–32.

Moulaert, Frank, Flavia Martinelli, Sara González, and Erik Swyngedouw. 2007. Introduction: Social Innovation and Governance in European Cities. *European Urban and Regional Studies* 14 (3) (July 25): 195–209.

Mumford, Michael D., Ginamarie M. Scott, Blaine Gaddis, and Jill M. Strange. 2002. Leading Creative People: Orchestrating Expertise and Relationships. *Leadership Quarterly* 13 (6): 705–750.

Nicholls, Alex, Julie Simon, and Madeleine Gabriel (eds.). 2015. *New Frontiers in Social Innovation Research*. London, UK: Palgrave Macmillan.

Nicolaides, Aliki, and Victoria J. Marsick. 2016. Understanding Adult Learning in the Midst of Complex Social 'Liquid Modernity'. *New Directions for Adult and Continuing Education* 2016 (149) (March): 9–20.

Pascale, Richard T., Jerry Sternin, and Monique Sternin. 2010. *The Power of Positive Deviance: How Unlikely Innovators Solve the World's Toughest Problems*. Boston, MA: Harvard Business Review Press.

Peterson, Christopher, and Martin Seligman. 2004. *Character Strengths and Virtues: A Handbook and Classification*, 1st ed. New York, NY: American Psychological Association and Oxford University Press.

Peterson, Gayle, Robert M. Yawson, John Sherman, and Ivy Johnson Kanda. 2018. A Systems Model of Using the Deliberate Leadership® Framework for

Addressing Wicked Problems. *International Journal of Business and Systems Research* 12 (3): 262–289.
Ramírez, Rafael, and Cynthia Selin. 2014. Plausibility and Probability in Scenario Planning. *Foresight* 16 (1): 54–74.
Ramirez, Rafael, Malobi Mukherjee, Simona Vezzoli, and Arnoldo Matus Kramer. 2015. Scenarios as a Scholarly Methodology to Produce 'Interesting Research'. *Futures* 71: 70–87.
Santos, Filipe, Anne-Claire Pache, and Christoph Birkholz. 2015. Making Hybrids Work: Aligning Business Models and Organizational Design for Social Enterprises. *California Management Review* 57 (3): 36–58.
Seibert, S.E., M.L. Kraimer, and R.C. Liden. 2001. A Social Capital Theory of Career Success. *Academy of Management Journal* 44 (2) (April 1): 219–237.
Senge, P., B. Smith, N. Kruschwitz, J. Laur, and S. Schley. 2010. *The Necessary Revolution: Working Together to Create a Sustainable World*. New York, NY: Crown Publishing Group.
Shahzad, Khuram, and Alan R. Muller. 2016. An Integrative Conceptualization of Organizational Compassion and Organizational Justice: A Sensemaking Perspective. *Business Ethics* 25 (2): 144–158.
Shearer, Allan W. 2004. Applying Burke's Dramatic Pentad to Scenarios. *Futures* 36 (8): 823–835.
Threlfall, Valerie. 2013. *Landscape Review of the Beneficiary Feedback Field*, December 8. Prepared for Fay Twersky, Lindsay Louie, and Colleagues of the Effective Philanthropy Group.
Twersky, Fay, Phil Buchanan, and Valerie Threlfall. 2013. Listening to Those Who Matter Most, the Beneficiaries. *Stanford Social Innovation Review* 11 (2): 41–45.
Van Velsor, Ellen, and Cynthia McCauley. 2004. Our View of Leadership Development. In *The Center for Creative Leadership Handbook for Leadership Development*, 2nd ed., ed. C.D. McCauley and E. Van Velsor, 1–22. San Francisco, CA: Jossey-Bass.
Waddock, Sandra A., and James E. Post. 1995. Catalytic Alliances for Social Problem Solving. *Human Relations* 48 (8): 951–973.
Williams, Kate, and J.C. Durrance. 2008. Social Networks and Social Capital: Rethinking Theory in Community Informatics. *The Journal of Community Informatics* 4 (3): 1–20.
Yawson, Robert M. 2013. Systems Theory and Thinking as a Foundational Theory in Human Resource Development—A Myth or Reality? *Human Resource Development Review* 12 (1) (March 17): 53–85.
Yawson, Robert M. 2015. The 'Wicked Problem Construct' for Organisational Leadership and Development. *International Journal of Business and Systems Research* 9 (1): 67–85.

Yawson, Robert M., and Bradley C. Greiman. 2014. Stakeholder Analysis as a Tool for Systems Approach Research in HRD. In *Leading Human Resource Development through Research. Proceedings of the 21st Annual AHRD International Research Conference in the Americas*, ed. Julie Gedro, Diane D. Chapman, and Kate Guerdat, 1–28. Houston, TX: Academy of Human Resource Development.

Yawson, Robert M., Gayle Peterson, and Ivy Johnson Kanda. 2020. Collective Impact: Dialogue at the Interface of the Colliding Systems of Philanthropy. *World Review of Entrepreneurship, Management and Sustainable Development* 16 (1) (January): 1–24.

Zhang, L. 2014. Creative Educational Leadership: A Practical Guide to Leadership as Creativity. *Educational Management Administration & Leadership* 42 (1): 159–160.

Zulueta, Paquita de. 2015. Developing Compassionate Leadership in Health Care: An Integrative Review. *Journal of Healthcare Leadership* 8 (December): 1–10.

CHAPTER 3

Promise and Peril of Big Finance

Big Finance and Sustainability

Like the creation of the Wicked Problem framework, the genesis of capital for social purpose was born out of the tumultuous times of the 60s and 70s. Citizen activism and unrest around the Vietnam War; civil, environmental, and women's rights movements; and the anti-nuclear and South Africa anti-apartheid movements catalyzed transformative thinking around the role of business and society. Business schools debated the role of socially responsible business. Conservative University of Chicago economist Milton Friedman espoused a philosophy that the best way for business to be responsible was to increase profits and shareholder value; anything else would be irresponsible. But by the early 80s, Milton Moskowitz (a graduate of the University of Chicago) was advocating that the greatest companies were committed to business and society. He published, *The 100 Best Companies to Work for in America* and provided annual updates to *Fortune Magazine*.

The original version of this chapter was revised: Belated corrections have been updated. The correction to this chapter is available at https://doi.org/10.1007/978-3-030-40712-4_7

G. Peterson et al., *Navigating Big Finance and Big Technology for Global Change*, Palgrave Studies in Impact Finance,
https://doi.org/10.1007/978-3-030-40712-4_3

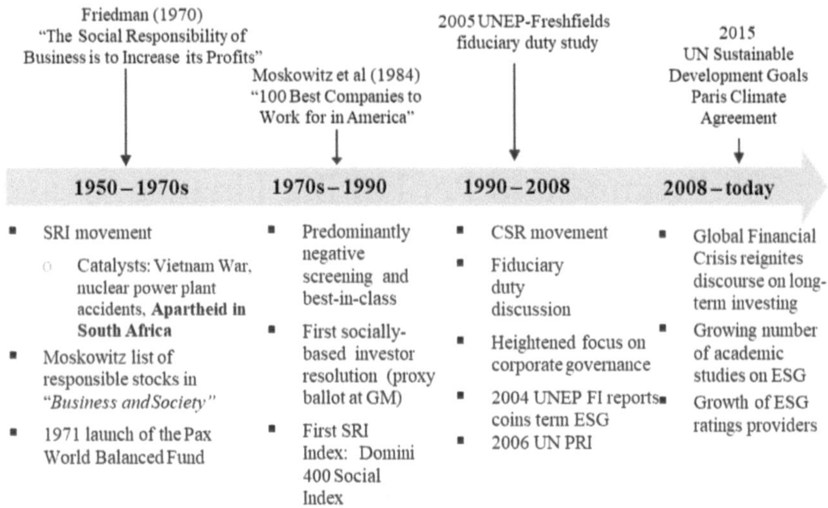

Fig. 3.1 Milestones of social responsible investing and ESG (*Source* Adapted from Amel-Zadeh 2019)

During this same time, Ford, MacArthur, and W. K. Kellogg foundations launched program-related investments using grantmaking to test the financial tools of debt capital, equity, and guarantees to philanthropy.

Oxford scholar Amir Amel-Zadeh's summarizes the evolution of a socially responsible investing movement and milestones in Fig. 3.1.

In 1998, the Aspen Institute founded its Business and Society Program working with business executives and scholars to align business decisions and investments with the long-term health of society and the planet. The program was designed to "challenge conventional ideas about capitalism and markets, to test new measures of business success and to connect classroom theory and business practice."

The 2000s ushered in a robust Corporate Social Responsibility movement and the United Nations Global Compact was created to support responsible corporate sustainability. In 2004, the United Nations Environment Programme (UNEP) Finance Initiative coined the term ESG (Environmental, Social, and Governance) and in 2006 the UN Principles of Responsible Investing (UNPRI) were established. Launched at the New York Stock Exchange, the Principles for Responsible Investment are "a voluntary and aspirational set of investment principles that offer a menu of possible actions for incorporating ESG issues into investment practice" (PRI 2019). Today 450 of the 2300-plus PRI signatories have over $1.3 trillion in assets linked UNPRI-related investments (IFC 2019b).

In 2015, UNPRI, UNEP, and Generation Foundation launched a three-year project, *Fiduciary Duty in The 21st Century-Global Statement on Investor Obligations and Duties*, to clarify investors' obligations around incorporating ESG (Environmental, Social, and Governance) issues into investment practices (Sullivan et al. 2019). The project published a global statement of investors' obligations and duties, roadmaps in more than 10 countries on policy changes required and research into investor obligations and duties in six Asian markets (Sullivan et al. 2019).

Again, like the Wicked Problems framework, supporters of SRI, UNPRI, ESG are diverse and vocal. Advocates for socially responsible investing include CEOs of large investment houses, corporations, foundations, civil society organizations, and government. Clients and citizens are calling for business to be more responsible and trustworthy in practice, helping protect the planet and end inequality. The World Economic Forum and the UN through the SDGs are amplifying the call for capital with purpose and performance measures.

According to the *Financial Times*, ESG has gone mainstream and ESG investments are making money. ESG-focused investments across asset classes do as well or better than markets' average returns (Holder 2019; Thompson 2018). Studies also show that sovereign debt risk is inversely related to ESG scores (Reznick et al. 2019). Estimates run between $20–30 trillion under ESG management in 2018, up from $16 trillion in 2016 and with $35 trillion projected for 2020 (McGrath 2019). While this is a lot of money, relative to the estimated total market of $269 trillion in investable assets (IFC Appendix B 2019a), ESG-related investing comprises around 8.6% (IFC 2019b). Nonetheless, naysayers who predicted that ESG would collapse at the first sign of trouble in the markets, seem to have been proved wrong during the COVID-19 pandemic during which ESG investing has stayed strong (Mooney 2020). According to Morningstar, ESG investment funds in the United Kingdom enjoyed their second highest quarter for inflows during the first three months of 2020, and despite a fall in March as the pandemic hit home, inflows had recovered by April (Mooney 2020).

Figure 3.2 defines the three facets of ESG—environment, social, and governance.

Interest in ESG investments is growing across the globe. At the beginning of 2018, Europe led the way in terms of gross ESG assets (US$14,765 billion) followed by the US (US$11,995 billion) followed by Canada, Australia and Japan (Fig. 3.3).

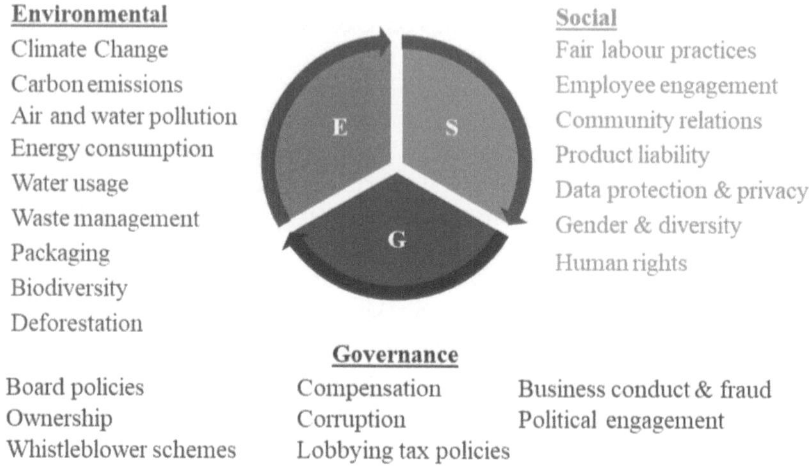

Fig. 3.2 ESG categories (*Source* Adapted from Amel-Zadeh [2019])

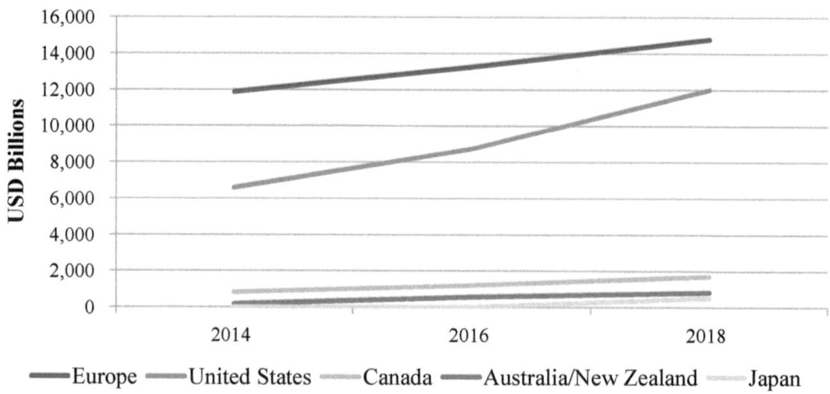

Fig. 3.3 Growth in ESG assets by region 2014–2018 (*Source* Adapted from Global Sustainable Investment Alliance's 2018 Global Sustainable Investment Review; conversion to US currency based on currency exchanges as of 31 December 2017)

ESG Challenges

These are promising signs of a growing movement, and a sense that companies with strong ESG performance are better able to ride out the kind of crisis the COVID-19 pandemic represents (Mooney 2020). But there are still red flags waving for the field. Research by Amel-Zadeh shows several obstacles and perils in ESG investment practice (Amel-Zadeh 2019). As shown in Fig. 3.4, the top areas of concern for the field include: lack of compatibility across firms; lack of reporting standards; the cost of gathering and analyzing ESG data; nonfinancial disclosures are too general; and the lack of quantifiable nonfinancial information and lack of comparability over time.

Lack of Compatibility

When it comes to what is meant by ESG, the lack of compatibility across firms is significant. And there are a lot of firms that have developed and continue to refine their own factors, and rating and reporting systems, e.g., Bloomberg ESG Data Service, Institutional Shareholder Services (ISS), MSCI, Sustainalytics Company, and Thomson Reuters ESG (Huber and Comstock 2017). Moreover, most of the large asset managers (e.g., BlackRock, Vanguard Asset Management, State Street

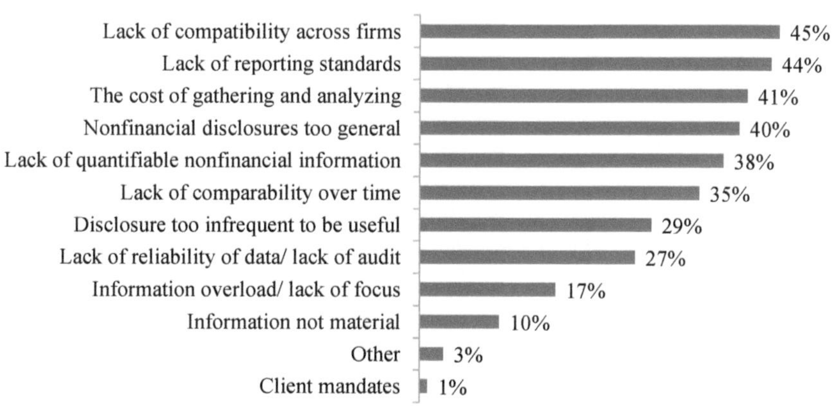

Fig. 3.4 Challenges of ESG Mainstream (*Source* Adapted from Amel-Zadeh [2019])

Global Advisors, Fidelity Investments, and J.P. Morgan Asset Management) have their own proprietary ESG rating systems.

The Exxon–Tesla Challenge: Which One Is a Better ESG Investment?

How does the lack of compatibility, reporting standards, quantifiable and nonquantifiable reporting data manifest itself in these challenges? Imagine that you are an investor that wants to make money and support organizations that have a high ESG rating. Who would you invest in: Exxon Mobile or Tesla?

The obvious answer would seem to be Tesla with its strong foothold in emissions-free transport. ExxonMobil or Exxon, by contrast, would appear to be part of the high polluting, hydrocarbon based economy that advocates of sustainability would like to come to a close. The *Wall Street Journal* compared the ESG ratings of Tesla and Exxon (among others) by three major rating firms—FTSE Russell, MSCI and Sustainalytics (Mackintosh 2018). The ratings—overall and by E, S, and G—vary significantly (Fig. 3.5).

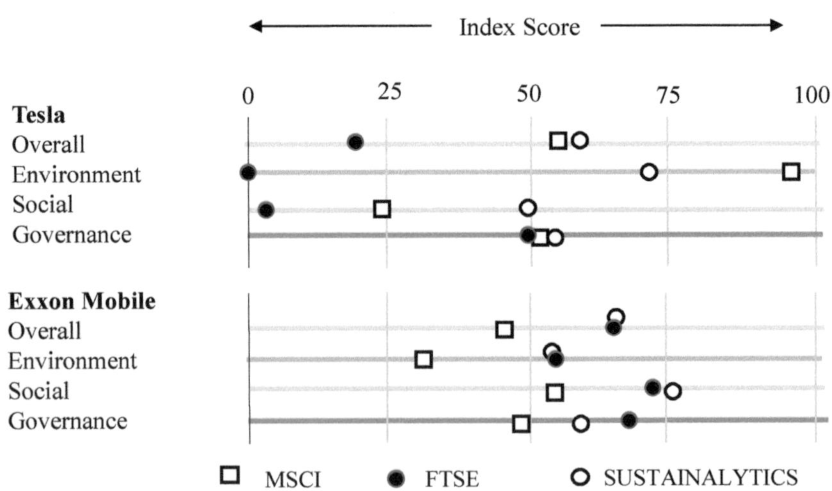

Fig. 3.5 T and exxon ESG scores: comparison by rating firm (*Source* Adapted from Amel-Zadeh [2019])

Depending on the firm, Tesla either ranked at the top of the industry (MSCI), somewhere in the middle (Sustainalytics), or at the bottom of carmakers (FTSE). Why the disparities? FTSE Russell, MSCI and Sustainalytics each have different rating systems (Mackintosh 2018). Each measured different aspects of Tesla and weighted differently the ones they all measured. For example, "MSCI gives Tesla a near-perfect score for environment, because it has selected two themes as the most important for the car industry: the carbon produced by its products, and the opportunities the company has in clean technology. FTSE gives Tesla a "zero" on environment, because its scores ignore emissions from the company's cars, rating only emissions from its factories ..." Lack of disclosure by Tesla on social issues is another factor behind the very different scores. If no information is provided, FTSE "assumes the worst." Whereas "MSCI is more generous, assuming that if there's no disclosure the company operates in line with regional and industry norms."

The three firms rating ExxonMobil exemplify the lack of standardization in compiling the three dimensions—E, S, and G—into a composite score. Does one of the three factors get more weight? One firm, Sustainalytics, rated Exxon the highest "... because it puts a 40 percent weight on social issues, where Exxon does well thanks to strong policies for its workers, supply chain, and local communities." MSCI, however, puts more weight on the E factor (51%) and less on the S factor (17%), thus ranking Exxon lower.

Overall, Exxon appears to rate higher on ESG than Tesla.

Let's scratch beyond the ratings. As an investor interested investing in companies with high environmental, social, and financial returns how would you feel if you discovered during due diligence the following information about Exxon and Tesla.

Exxon is being sued by several state and city governments seeking compensation for climate change damages. Internal Exxon documents disclosed that the oil company understood the science of global warming; predicted its dangerous consequences; and spent millions knowingly misleading the public on its contributions to climate change.

In April 2020, Moody's Investor Service downgraded ExxonMobil's rating from Aaa to Aa1, following a long period of concern about negative cash flow. Low prices for oil and diminished refining and chemical earnings have caused ExxonMobil's rising capital expenditures and weak revenues. In theory, ESG ratings would also be impacted. The E is related to potential carbon dioxide regulations, but also include natural and man-made hazards. Social risks are related to demographic and societal trends. Demand for oil, gas, and refined products could accelerate the pace of energy transitions or changes in technology that affect demand for hydrocarbon represent a material and growing risk for the company.

Exxon has a history of contesting environmental remediation efforts, including suits like the Exxon Valdez oil spill in which 11 million gallons of crude oil was spilled into Alaska's Prince William Sound killing hundreds of thousands of animals and fouling more than 1000 miles of coastline (Taylor 2014). For more than 20 years, Exxon waged a legal battle to reduce a civil settlement with fishermen and impacted communities from $5 billion to $500 million. Because of the long delay, more than one-third of the fishermen had died.

Unlike its peers at Royal Dutch Shell, Exxon is not actively investing in alternative energy. Table 3.1 shows how it compares to other oil and gas companies are making the shift to renewable energy. Exxon is investing in oil exploration, fracking, and oil sands even though the use of those reserves threatens to push the temperature of the planet to 4° Celsius (Pickl 2019).

Let's turn to Tesla.

In early 2019, Tesla has been found guilty of federal hazardous waste violations at their automobile manufacturing plant in Fremont, California (Egelko 2019). The settlement required Tesla to purchase $55,000 in emergency response equipment and pay a $31,000 penalty. Worker safety is also an issue. Investigative reporting reveals ongoing safety concerns such as back strain, repetitive-stress injuries, and severe headaches (Evans and Perry 2018). It notes that Tesla's injury rate exceeded the industry average in 2016 and that the company had chosen not to report certain incidents as required under California labor law. Recall from Chapter 1 T's involvement in a lawsuit with other tech companies about the illegal use of child labor in securing precious metals such as cobalt in the DRC.

Yet, Tesla remains a vibrant company with significant revenues. Through the end of the third quarter in 2019, it had over $17 billion in revenue (Tesla 2019). Though it had a net loss of $907 million for the year, its third-quarter profits of $254 million sent its shares up more than 20% (Tesla 2019; Kolodny 2019).

During the same period, ExxonMobil reported a 49% decline in third-quarter earnings on lower oil prices and higher costs. The company reported 75 cents in earnings and $65.05 billion in revenue, which did top analyst expectations. According to Chairman and CEO Darren

Table 3.1 Comparison oil and gas companies renewable energy investments

Assessment criteria	*Weigh (%)*	*Shell*	*ExxonMobil*	*Chevron*	*Total*	*BP*	*Eni*	*Petrobas*	*Equinor*
Hydro	5	0	0	0	1	0	0	1	0
Solar	5	1	0	1	1	1	1	1	1
Wind	5	1	0	1	1	1	1	1	1
Biofuels		1	1	0	1	1	1	0	0
Carbon Capture	5	1	1	1	1	1	1	0	1
Geothermal		0	0	0	0	0	0	0	0
Energy Storage/EV Charging		1	0	0	1	1	0	0	1
Explicit Renewable Strategy/Renewable Capital Allocation	5	1	0	0	1	1	1	0	1
Capital Investment into Renewables (billion $ per year)	50	1	0	0	0.5	0.5	0.3	0	0.5
Dedicated Renewable Team	5	1	0	0	1	1	1	0	1
Renewable Venture Capital Arm	5	1	0	1	1	1	1	0	1
Total score	100	9	2	4	9.5	8.5	7.3	3	7.5
Total weighted (%)		90	10	20	70	65	50	15	60

Source Adapted from Pickl, Energy Strategy Reviews 26 (2019)

Woods, the company is "Making excellent progress on our long-term growth strategy" (Stevens 2019). Shares of the United States's largest oil company gained 3% after Woods' announcement.

These examples are not outliers or based on older efforts. A September 2019 report from InfluenceMap indicates ongoing issues with the energy sector and ESGs. Assessing the presence of fossil fuel reserves owned by the companies held by 118 climate-themed ESG funds with an aggregate asset under management (AUM) of US$18B, the report found dramatic variation (InfluenceMap 2019). At one extreme, it found two funds (each with over $100M in AUM) marketed by Asia-based Fullgoal and Lion Fund Management companies had holdings of Chinese mining companies like Shaanxi Coal and Yanzhou Coal Mining. Its research also identified two State Street funds marketed as "fossil fuel reserves free" and based on MSCI indices, which have stakes in major energy and mining companies active in thermal coal, including RWE, Vale and Sasol. The report concludes by stating, "There remains huge variation in the terms used to market funds as climate themed, including 'low carbon,' 'climate aware,' and 'fossil fuel free.' Clear discrepancies between these labels and fund contents (for instance, the presence of coal mining companies in 'fossil fuel reserve free' funds) indicate that more stringent advertising standards may be pertinent" (InfluenceMap 2019). The two ESG examples provided later in this chapter delve further into the climate aspects of ESG and climate funds.

The lesson? Due diligence on ESG is essential yet can be insufficient to produce a picture of environmental, social, or governance performance in line with what people might expect to be good practice.

Lack of Standard Rules

Often touted is the fact that "38 of the largest 50 economies in the world have, or are developing, disclosure requirements for corporations covering environmental, social and governance issues" (Heath et al. 2016). That is a good first step: however, many of the largest economies remain at the development stage, or have what Agnes Neher of J. Safra Sarasin Bank calls "soft" or voluntary requirements (Neher 2017).

The two largest countries and regions for ESG funds—the EU and the United States—are at very different stages of development and are developing different approaches to disclosure (Langenbucher 2018). The

EU already has several "hard rules," with more in development (Langenbucher 2018). In the United States, sixty-eight organizations and individuals, including state pension funds, state treasuries, and asset managers, petitioned the US Securities Exchange Commission in October 2018 to develop rules (Williams and Fisch 2018). The authors summarized the need for such standards:

> Without adequate standards, more and more public companies are voluntarily producing 'sustainability reports' designed to explain how they are creating long-term value. There are substantial problems with the nature, timing, and extent of these voluntary disclosures, however. Thus, we respectfully ask the Commission to engage in notice and comment rulemaking to develop a comprehensive framework for clearer, more consistent, more complete, and more easily comparable information relevant to companies' long-term risks and performance.

Timothy Doyle of the American Council for Capital Formation (ACCF), raises deeper concerns about the current system's ability to generate very different rating results. "Individual agencies' ESG ratings can vary dramatically. An individual company can carry vastly divergent ratings from different agencies simultaneously, due to differences in methodology, subjective interpretation, or an individual agency's agenda. There are also inherent biases: from market cap size, to location, to industry or sector – all rooted in a lack of uniform disclosure" (Doyle 2018). Furthering the need for standardization is the concern that the ratings industry may have conflicts of interest similar to those reported with proxy advisors. Doyle summarizes,

> [A]sset manager reliance on outsourced data, to comply with their fiduciary duty or new mandates, is similar to the rise of the proxy advisory industry. Many of the lacking elements within the proxy advisory industry (i.e., transparency, oversight, and unaudited disclosures) are also present in the ESG ratings industry.

There are various ongoing attempts to foster a more uniform understanding of ESG. These include, but are not limited to, common principles/standards of the kind advocated through the Global Reporting Initiative, the SDGs and the Future-Fit Foundation benchmark discussed in Chapter 6. Standardization is fostered indirectly through initiatives such as the collaboration between MIT's Presencing Institute and HuffPost so that the latter's multimedia platform can be used to raise awareness about the changing nature of capitalism, and develop a rigorous discourse about what this involves. It promises to illuminate the environmental, social, and economic costs of capitalism's current course; to illustrate the principles and practices that make change happen; and to showcase the inspiring stories and strategies that are moving new economy models from the margins into the mainstream. A different approach to engendering standardization is being taken by the Well-being Economy Alliance, and the Well-being Economy Governments partnership (WEGo) in particular, a collaboration of national and regional governments promoting and sharing expertise and transferrable policy practices in order to deepen their understanding and advance their shared ambition of building well-being economies. Participating governments include Scotland, New Zealand, Iceland, and Wales. Other examples include initiatives such as Positive Money which is pushing central banks to align their policies with sustainability, and Climate Safe Lending which seeks to align European and North American bank lending with the goals of the Paris Climate Accord to keep the planet well below a 1.5° Celsius temperature rise.

What Is not Included

Other ESG perils beyond the lack of standardization limit the current ESG's credibility. Some may be fixable; others may be inherent to the financial system's narrow view of risks.

Lack of Adequate "S" and "G" Metrics

The "S" in ESG (i.e., social) remains the most challenging in that social dimensions of sustainability are not always as easy to quantify as the other two dimensions. Moreover, the majority of social factors assessed in the ratings focus on internal issues like company policies and training, and not on external issues affecting the communities in which the companies or investments are occurring. A 2017 study by New York University's Stern Center for Business and Human Rights found that:

> [S]ocial measurement prioritized internal procedures over those that involved external stakeholder participation. Over half of all indicators

> (58 percent) evaluated either the governance structures a company has in place for social issues (e.g., roles, management systems, policies, and commitments) or its information gathering and assessment processes (e.g., audits and external assurance, risk or impact assessments, and general data gathering efforts). Less than 20 percent of indicators examined either stakeholder engagement or remedial mechanisms. (O'Connor and Labowitz 2017)

Furthermore, the same study found that much of the social measures focused on activities or efforts rather than on outcomes or effects.

> Only 8 percent of the more than 1700 'S' indicators we examined evaluated the effects of company practices. Rather, a significant majority of indicators (92 percent) measured company efforts and activities, such as issuing policies or commitments; conducting audits, risk assessments, or training; participating in membership organizations or other collaborations; or engaging stakeholders. (O'Connor and Labowitz 2017)

Capturing What Happens in Supply Chains

It is not just the ESG of the target company that needs to be considered but also the ESG of its suppliers. Two critical supply chain issues are labor (part of the "S") and environmental impact.

Labor. The complexity of global supply chains along with the lax enforcement of labor laws in many countries have helped enable forced labor. Today, forced labor affects an estimated 25 million people worldwide (International Labor Organization). A significant number of people in conditions of modern-day slavery are employed in the supply chains of global industries, from electronics and apparel to primary commodities like palm oil and seafood. In some places, slavery is passed down through generations—notably South Asia's centuries-old practices of bonded labor, where debts pass down from parent to child (pfc social impact advisors-Humanity United 2018a).

Currently, ESG ratings inadequately capture slave labor in a company's supply chains, especially past their first-tier suppliers; tracking further down the chain has proven to be difficult. A recent multilateral effort, the Global Fund to End Modern Slavery (Global Fund, or GFEMS), announced at the January 2018 World Economic Forum should help. One of its three interconnected goals is to "create value by eliminating forced labor from supply chains at local, national, and international levels, as well as provide alternatives for vulnerable individuals" (Global Fund to End Modern Slavery).

Short of slave labor are the 700 million working poor (those earning below US$3.10 /day in terms of purchasing power parity) and the 1.4 billion workers in "vulnerable employment," i.e., without formal work arrangements, inadequate earnings, difficult working conditions, and inadequate social security, voice and representation by trade unions and similar organizations (International Labour Organization 2018).

Environment. Many companies rely on natural resources either directly or indirectly. This natural capital—clean air and water, land, fertile soil, biodiversity, and geological resources—has an estimated value of up to $72 trillion per year (The Corporate ECO Forum and The Nature Conservancy 2012). UNEP reports that we are spending this natural capital at around $6.6 trillion per year (PRI Association and UNEP Finance Initiative 2011). Yet, the ESG ratings do not fully account for such costs. In the *2018 State of Green Business*, Joel Makower notes,

> If companies had to internalize all of the natural capital costs associated with their business, for example as a result of increased regulations or new carbon taxes, their profit would be greatly at risk. The natural capital cost generated by the largest 1200 companies in the world is nearly two times higher than their net income. (Makower 2018)

Furthermore, Makower continues, much of these natural capital costs are embedded in supply chains. "On average, 79 percent of company impacts are in their supply chain. For this reason, measuring impacts from goods and services purchased by companies is essential in understanding their natural capital costs and exposure to environmental regulation and policy risks."

ESG and Tales of Two Climate-Focused Investors

Making Money Through Mission: ESG and Climate as Risk Management

We have presented data to suggest that ESG investment is not only on the increase but looks robust when confronted by sustainability challenges. Away from the statistics, another perspective is provided by investors themselves. Thomas Van Dyck has been active in social and responsible investing for 35 years starting with his work to help the South Africa divestment movement. He is one of the founding members of the Divest Invest Movement, and is a founder and board member of As You Sow, a shareholder action group and environmental foundation.

Using climate investments as an example, Van Dyck offers a rationale for Big Finance to embrace ESG. He describes the potential for reduced risk and better long-term financial and nonfinancial gains when ESG factors are appropriately incorporated into investment analyses. Not attending to ESG, he notes, can mean foregoing investment opportunities, such as in alternative energy companies or underestimating the speed with which existing technologies can be disintermediated by new technologies, which "experts" have a track record of doing.

Van Dyck got into socially responsible investing in its infancy because of his passion for the environment and justice. In the 1980s, Desmond Tutu was for global action on Apartheid in South Africa through the divestment movement. As a young investment advisor, Van Dyck and many investors wanted to take action too. Through research and advocacy, he and his partner at the time, Ted Barone, documented how the California State Teachers Retirement System (CALSTRS) could divest from South Africa. CALSTRS did divest, and Nelson Mandela and Rev. Desmond Tutu credited the divestment movement as one of the important factors in the fall of apartheid.

Galvanized by the push to divest from Apartheid, Van Dyck and a small group of others formed a circle to grow socially responsible investing in the United States. The circle included people such as Amy Domini, Peter Kinder, Steve Lydenberg of KLD and the Domini Index, Wayne Silby of the Calvert Group, Tim Smith of ICCR (Interfaith Committee on Corporate Responsibility), John Harrington, and other frontline groups who have led the way to push investments to help build global justice. They were joined by foundation leaders: Steve Viederman of Jessie Smith Noyes, John Powers of The Educational Foundation of America, Adelaide Gomer, and later the Park Foundation, and celebrities who were early adopters of aligning their money with their values. This group would become leaders of the movement that has evolved into ESG investing.

As their group began to see what was happening to the climate and our planet, there was a new call to action. Desmond Tutu wrote in *The Guardian* in 2014, "we need an apartheid-style boycott to save the planet" (Tutu 2014). Executive Director Ellen Dorsey of Wallace Global Foundation wondered why there wasn't a divestment movement on fossil fuels, and moved to form the Divest Invest movement (pfc social impact advisors-Wallace Global, 2018b).

Van Dyck's team was asked to look at the financial impacts of divesting from fossil fuel. What they found was that beyond the moral reasons to push for change, there was an incredible amount of financial issues with the whole fossil fuel sector. They discovered three important ideas. First, the entire energy sector is underperforming. Second, the shift away from a fossil fuel economy is a shift in innovation, and innovation often happens exponentially faster than expected. Third, there are important drivers in growing a new energy economy for the United States and other countries. We examine these individually below.

The Energy Sector Is a Chronic Underperformer

Van Dyck points out that many finance experts might argue, "you can't wipe out the entire energy sector of the S&P 500 from your portfolio, because you'll lose diversity, you'll increase your risk, and you'll lower your expected return." They are correct in one regard: diversifying your portfolio by asset class and by sectors is, for the most part, critical to generating long-term outperformance. However, the energy sector has issues with long-term performance, and therefore this logic does not apply. As such, in addition to their moral opposition to owning fossil fuels, many investors began to question why a sector that is underperforming was still in their portfolio.

Van Dyck notes that the S&P 500 energy sector does not have a single renewable energy company, only oil and gas companies. Moreover, looking at a full market cycle, from the peak of the market in 2007, before the Great Recession, up through the second quarter of 2019, the energy sector is the worst performing sector in the S&P (see Table 3.2). The energy sector has had a total (non-annualized) return of 7.7%. The entire S&P has more than doubled over that same time frame, with a total return of 141.4%. Furthermore, if you look back to the market bottom, in 2009, until the end of the second quarter 2019, energy was up 97.3% while the S&P 500 was up over 400%.

A comparison of the S&P 500 and the performance of XLE, an index fund tracking the energy sector of the S&P 500, also shows the underperformance of oil and gas. Between 2007 and 2012, oil and gas was broadly aligned with S&P 500 as a whole; but from 2013 onwards, the former considerably and consistently underperformed the latter. Table 3.3 shows

Table 3.2 Non-annualized returns (percentage) by selected sectors

	Financials	*Energy*	*Technology*	*Health care*	*Utilities*	*S&P 500*
June 2019	17.2	13.1	27.1	8.1	14.7	18.5
Since market peak (October 2007)	21.1	7.7	279.0	219.5	128.0	141.4
Since market low (March 2009)	560.9	97.3	694.2	415.1	299.1	439.5

Source Adapted from FactSet, Russell Investment Group, Standard and Poor's, and J.P. Morgan Asset Management

Table 3.3 Risk adjusted returns 2007–2019: ESG manager, XLE, and S&P

	Sustainable global equities manager	*XLE*	*S&P 500*
Return (%)	10.2	0.61	8.32
Cumulative excess return (%)	52.6	−138.56	–
Std. dev (%)	16.48	24.87	16.58
Sharpe ratio	0.5871	0.0033	0.4699
Information ratio	0.27	−0.49	–
Tracking error vs. Mkt (%)	7.0057	15.5787	0
Upside capture	99	82.5	–
Downside capture	83.4	135.6	–

Source StyleAdvisor. For information purposes only. Past performance does not indicate future results

the extent of underperformance, not only compared to the S&P 500, but also ESG indexes. It demonstrates that not only is the absolute return of the ESG Manager better than the energy sector of the S&P 500, but the risk adjusted return is better, too.

Energy is also the most volatile sector of all the S&P 500 sectors, and it tends to fall harder than other sectors (Table 3.4). Investors in the energy sector are getting less return than other sectors with more risk. That should be the opposite of one's goal. This is why those who divested over five years ago have enhanced their returns.

Table 3.4 Annual returns for S&P 500 and S&P sectors: 2015–2018

	2018	*2017*	*2016*	*2015*	*5-year annualized*
S&P 500	−4.40	21.82	11.95	1.37	8.49
Consumer discretionary	0.80	22.98	6.03	10.11	9.69
Consumer staples	−8.40	13.49	5.38	6.60	6.26
Energy	−18.10	- 1.01	27.36	−21.12	−5.56
Financials	−13.00	22.14	22.75	- 1.56	8.16
Health care	6.50	22.08	−2.69	6.89	11.12
Industrials	−13.10	21.01	18.85	−2.56	5.95
Materials	−14.70	23.84	16.69	−8.38	3.84
Real estate	−2.20	10.85	1.12	1.24	8.84
Tech	−2.30	38.83	13.85	5.92	14.93
Telecom	−12.50	- 1.25	23.49	3.40	3.90
Utilities	4.10	12.11	16.29	−4.84	10.74
BCGI	0.88	2.14	2.08	1.07	1.85

Source RBC Wealth Management, Bloomberg; S&P Dow Jones Indices; total-return data. 5-Year Annualized 2013–2018

The Experts Are Often Wrong

Thirty-four years ago, Van Dyck was an anti-nuclear power activist on the East Coast. He worked for the Fund for Secure Energy and raised money for media campaigns to close down nuclear power plants. Back then, the industry experts said nuclear power was too cheap to be metered. As with nuclear power, industry experts consistently underestimate the power of disruption and how quickly it can take place. As such, industry experts have a track record of making very bad predictions. Like the time in 1985 when McKinsey and AT&T predicted that by the year 2000 there would be over 900,000 cell phone subscribers. The actual number? 109 million. They were off by a factor of 120 times. Not a small miss in only 15 years.

In estimating disruption, the experts don't only get the order of magnitude wrong. They also get the pace wrong. When technology disrupts an industry, it happens much quicker than what the experts expect. Imagine a picture of Fifth Avenue, Manhattan on Easter morning 1900. Between the columns of pedestrians along the sidewalks, the horse and buggy dominates the streets. In fact, you would be lucky to see a single automobile. But just 13 years later, a photo taken from the same position would present a very different picture. Instead of horses, the street would be filled with cars: it was as if the horse and buggy had become extinct. That is rapid change indeed.

Another example is when digital imaging entered the film era. Eastman Kodak, remember it? It used to be a Dow Jones industrial company with a $30 billion market cap (Gara and Deaux 2013). The digital camera came into place in 1999, then the smartphone, and nine years later, in 2012, Eastman Kodak declared bankruptcy after 131 years in business (Gara and Deaux 2013; Zhang 2017; De La Merced 2012).

Even within the cell phone industry: Nokia and Blackberry were early movers in bringing cell phones to the masses. When the first iPhone was launched in 2007, Blackberry—business's cell phone of choice—had a market cap of over $40 billion, and Nokia—the world's most popular cell phone—had a cap of $144.5 billion. Over the next half a decade, Apple launched iPhones 3g to 5, and by the time iPhone 5s/5c came out, Blackberry's market cap had slumped to $5.4 billion while Nokia's was just $15.2 billion.

Technological Disruption in the Energy Sector

These examples show how rapidly change can take place, removing incumbent companies like a tornado can uproot a house. Why should renewable energy not be the next tornado? In fact, one can argue that it already is. General Electric, the global industrials conglomerate with sales strongly tied to the natural gas power generation market, has already felt the impact. From 2014 until early 2017, GE's stock price was broadly in step with the S&P 500. But its stock price declined massively after misjudging the demand for gas turbines, as well as the increasing affordability of alternative energy sources. By 2019, the price had fallen 64.6% compared to 2014, while the S&P 500 was up 43.1%.

Why is that happening? Because the cost of producing and storing renewable energy has been declining over this period, driving increased adoption of these energy sources. Solar power is at $0.04 a kilowatt hour, having fallen $0.02–$0.03 per year on average from 2006 to 2012 and $0.01 per year from 2013 to 2016 (Bolinger and Seel 2018). Wind power is at or below $0.02 a kilowatt hour, down from $0.07 in 2000 (Wiser and Bolinger 2017). Massive adoption of both solar and wind technologies has followed. And the cost of battery storage has dropped almost 76% since 2012 (Mai 2019). Why is that important? Because when the sun and wind produce more energy than you need, if you can store that electron in a battery, you can release it during those times when the sun isn't shining and the wind isn't blowing.

Additional Risks to Owning Carbon

In addition to the risk of technological disruption, which is one of the biggest risks to owning fossil fuels, here are five of the other main risks that Van Dyck uses to help people understand why divesting their portfolios from carbon can generate long term outperformance:

1. **Stranded asset risk**. This is addressed in the Carbon Tracker paper that Bill McKibben made famous in a Rolling Stone article that went viral called "Do the Math" (McKibben 2012). Carbon Tracker, a group of former oil analysts based in London, says that we have to keep 80% of the reserves currently reflected on the balance sheets of the oil companies in the ground in order to keep the temperature of the planet below the two degrees Celsius level required to avert climate catastrophe (Carbon Tracker Initiative 2011).

   Therefore, the question we should be asking is: are the oil companies going to be allowed to burn that 80% of their reserves, and allow taxpayers and global citizens to bear the costs of the resulting climate change? Or are they going to be forced to keep those reserves in the ground? This is the battle being waged in many places. Those reserves are priced into their stock today as an asset available for extraction, which presents a risk from an investment perspective.
2. **Litigation risk**. Over the past few years, two states in the United States launched fraud investigations into Exxon over climate change, and one has followed with a lawsuit. Nine cities and counties, from New York to San Francisco, have sued major fossil fuel companies seeking compensation for climate change damages. And determined children have filed lawsuits against the federal government and various state governments, claiming the governments have an obligation to safeguard the environment. These suits remain ongoing, but we hope to see their outcomes follow in the footsteps of the lawsuits against the tobacco industry, where plaintiffs have seen increasing success in the last 20 years (Michon, undated). While the majority of climate cases are in the United States, such cases are expanding further afield: according to a recent report by the

Grantham Research Institute on Climate Change and the Environment at the London School of Economics, cases have been brought in at least 28 countries and have been spreading across Europe and the Asia/Pacific region (Drugmand 2019). That's a huge liability if you own fossil fuels.

3. **Regulatory risk**. Given the massive economic and societal impacts of climate change, in the right political environment, investors should be worried about what regulator might do to impact the flexibility of traditional energy companies. We know the current White House Administration has trumped the regulatory situation by gutting the EPA. Regulations, however, cannot stop technology innovation. It can slow it down, or speed it up, but it can't stop technology's disruption from taking place.
4. **Demand risk**. The oil companies think they're going to need to keep looking for supply until 2050. They don't think peak demand is going to happen. We think peak demand for oil is going to happen when we move to electric cars. California is considering legislation to accelerate the push to get 5 million electric cars on the roads by 2030 using tax credits. Nine states in the United States are planning on using 100% renewable energy by various target dates (Sierra Club, undated). Sweden is aiming to eliminate fossil fuels from electricity generation by 2040. Costa Rica is already 95% renewable and is aiming for 100% carbon neutrality by 2021. Nicaragua, Scotland, Germany, Uruguay, and Denmark are others hitting impressive milestones (The Climate Reality Project 2016).

The Externalities: Hidden Costs of Not Transitioning to Renewables

The costs of climate change—droughts, floods, fires, hurricanes, tornadoes, etc.,—exemplify the perils of not considering the wide ranging, immediate, and long- term impacts of investments. Moreover, they are climbing. In its 2018 report, Economic Losses, Poverty and Disasters 1998–2017, the UN Office for Disaster Risk Reduction states, "In 1998-2017 disaster-hit countries also reported direct economic losses valued at US$2908 billion, of which climate-related disasters caused US2,245 billion or 77 percent of the total. This is up from 68 percent (US$ 895 billion) of losses (US$ 1313 billion) reported between 1978 and 1997. Overall, reported losses from extreme weather events rose by 151 percent between these two 20-year periods."

Drivers of Investing in Renewable Energy

Now let's look at the five imperative reasons to invest sustainably in clean energy and related areas. Each relates to other ESG rating criteria.

1. **Global security**. Microgrids are much safer than centralized grids in two ways. The CIA and the FBI worry extensively about the centralized grid structure in the United States because it is easily hacked. Microgrids are much more difficult to hack. In addition, with centralized grids, accidents and impacts from climate disasters have far-reaching effects: Hurricane Maria took out power in Puerto Rico for up to 11 months in some parts of the country (Fernández Campbell 2018); when a tree fell across a power line in Ohio about 15 years ago, it set off a sequence of events that took out power for eight northeastern states for two days (Minkel 2008). More recently, the Camp Fire in California raged due to PG&E transmission lines (Eavis and Penn 2019). So microgrids from a national security perspective are much safer. The Planetary Security Initiative indicates that globally, climate change and the degradation of natural resources impact defense and foreign policy and missions in ways ranging from migration patterns, to conflict management over resource scarcity, or weaponizing, to changing demands on operational military capacity (van Reedt Dortland et al. 2019).
2. **Human Displacement**. According to a 2019 World Bank report, climate change may cause over 140 million people to be displaced before 2050 as families flee water scarcity, crop failure and rising sea levels. Much of this migration is expected to entail movement from rural areas to urban areas. As such, the World Bank "urged cities to prepare infrastructure, social services and employment opportunities ahead of the predicted influx" (Barron 2018).
3. **Jobs**. The 2019 National Solar Jobs Consensus found that there are more than 249,000 solar jobs in the United States (Solar Foundation 2020). Wind jobs amounted to 111,166 (National Association of State Energy Officials and Energy Futures Initiative 2018). Coal power generation jobs shrank by about 7%. The solar jobs are found in every single state and country (National Association of State Energy Officials and Energy Futures Initiative 2018). You don't need an oil reserve or a carbon reserve. They are in urban areas,

rural areas, in red states and blue states. These are high paying jobs and they'll be around for 20 or 30 years.

4. **Healthcare and other economic costs**. According to a report by the International Monetary Fund (IMF), as of 2015 there were $5.2 trillion in estimated annual subsidies provided to the global fossil fuel industry. Half of these were related to health impacts and lost work productivity (Coady et al. 2019).
5. **More predictable pricing.** Renewable energy costs do not fluctuate the way commodity prices do. Therefore, big companies are able to use renewable energy to better budget one of their main costs (RE100, undated). As such, we have seen major companies commit to going renewable as a business decision. It benefits employees and shareholders.

The Transition Is Coming

This transition to a clean energy economy is not just going to be in the solar and wind space: it's going to affect every single element of our economy. It's going to be in water infrastructure and pumping technology. It's going to be energy grid optimization, microgrids, battery storage. Transportation, sustainable buildings, LED lighting, HVAC systems, waste reduction, and agriculture. It's going to be across the entire global economy.

Investment and divestment fuel the transition including the Divest/Invest movement. Launched in 2014, it was organized by Divest Invest Philanthropy led by Wallace Global Foundation's Ellen Dorsey, The Park Foundation, University of Dayton, the Educational Foundation of America, Rockefeller Foundation and their grantees, Carbon Tracker, 350.org, As You Sow, and many more. At launch in 2014, asset owners and managers controlling $50 billion signed on to the movement, committing to divest from fossil fuels and invest in clean energy and sustainable business practices. As of August 2019, there was over $8.8 trillion of assets committed, and growing rapidly. A few recognizable signatories include The KR Foundation, The Church of Sweden, The Church of England, The Rockefeller Family Fund, the University of Oxford, the University of Cambridge, and the London School of Economics (DivestInvest 2018).

As the impacts from climate change continue to grow, Van Dyck predicts that the movement will also change. He believes that investors can help push for what is needed. It is possible.

Greta Thurnberg, a climate organizer has called all of us up to change:

> It is still not too late to act. It will take a far-reaching vision, it will take courage, it will take fierce, fierce determination to act now, to lay the foundations where we may not know all the details about how to shape the ceiling. In other words, it will take cathedral thinking. I ask you to please wake up and make changes required possible.

Hunter Lovins, American environmentalist, and co-founder of Rocky Mountain Institute added to Greta's call.

"A challenge to all of us. Be a worthy ancestor."

A "worthy ancestor" is one who takes necessary action even when they don't yet know the "shape of the ceiling." That might include the work of Majority Action which empowers shareholders to hold corporations accountable to high standards of corporate governance, social responsibility, and long-term value creation. Its Climate Majority Project educates and engages investors to transform the business models of the highest-carbon emitting companies by changing the composition, outlook, and practices of their governing boards to focus on climate change mitigation, adaptation, and resiliency. Equally, it might include nationalization of fossil fuel companies or reserves to avoid a potentially ruinous financial crisis caused by the bursting of the so-called "carbon bubble" as fossil fuels have to be kept in the ground. Understanding how to achieve this is part of the work of the Democracy Collaborative.

The Case of the McKnight Foundation Carbon Efficiency Strategy

The McKnight Foundation (McKnight), a fourth-generation family foundation based in Minnesota, has a mission to advance a more just, creative, and abundant future where people and planet thrive (McKnight Foundation 2018). Central to fulfilling its mission are two key programs focused on cutting carbon pollution in the Midwest and building a vibrant future of shared power, prosperity, and participation for all Minnesotans.

In 2014, McKnight committed to invest $200 million of its US$2.3 bn endowment in strategies that align with its mission. Investments aimed at generating a triple bottom line of financial, environmental and social returns, and were allocated across three classes, with 50% of the portfolio in lower-risk market return investments; 25% in investments with higher risk and lower possible financial returns; and 25% in program-related investments (PRIs) with returns running from zero to market rates (McKnight Foundation).

This commitment came from a history of innovative thinking, a Deliberate Leadership quality, about how to use resources more effectively. McKnight was one of the early adopters of program-related investments, beginning in the 1980s to support urban renewal and affordable housing with loans at below-market rates. Since 2008, McKnight has applied ISS (formerly RiskMetrics), a decision support tool for institutional investors, to vote proxies on its managed financial accounts, and has employed eight investment firms—representing over US$1.3 billion of its portfolio—who are signatories to the UN Principles for Responsible Investment (pfc social impact advisors 2016).

Rather than waiting for possible investments and products to appear, in late October 2014, McKnight launched the Carbon Efficiency Strategy (CES) with one of its assets managers, Mellon Capital Management (MCM), a wholly owned subsidiary of BNY Mellon, one of the world's largest and most established financial services firms. A portfolio of lower-carbon investments seeded by The McKnight Foundation, the CES product offered McKnight and other carbon-conscious investors a more proactive way to shift institutional investments toward companies whose practices could reduce carbon emissions exposure in investment portfolios.

The CES represented another milestone in McKnight's journey to, as Foundation President Kate Wolford says, "walk the talk" by aligning its programmatic and endowment investments with its mission. Wolford believes that the CES "helps fill a gap in the universe of investment products by demonstrating responsiveness to the demand by an institutional investor and sends a signal to the market about carbon emissions." CES investments, focused on one critical piece of the "E" of ESG, promise to reduce the Foundation's emissions-intensity profile in this particular investment account by more than 50% relative to investments with a more standard index exposure.

Building the CES portfolio proved a formidable task for McKnight, MCM (and its mothership BNY Mellon), and the other advisors McKnight brought to the table, including Mercer and Imprint Capital.

They learned that getting the right "standards" for creating an acceptable CES portfolio in terms of carbon reduction and market performance required several iterations and listening sessions.

Several issues required deeper dives into what McKnight really wanted and what its asset managers could deliver. As Wolford admits, "McKnight did not exactly know what success would look like when it embarked on this process." It knew it wanted a substantive product and not just window dressing. It knew it did not want to invest in any coal companies, but also saw that some companies with big carbon footprints had the opportunity to also make big carbon reductions. It did not want to have standards or screening processes that by definition excluded or biased against such companies. And it wanted to make sure that the CES portfolio did not track too far from the benchmarks it and its investment managers used to assess performance.

This learning and discovery were happening as MCM and the other advisors were trying to build the CES platform. The interim results revealed this dynamism. Regarding CES's second iteration Wolford observed, "It wasn't as robust as we had hoped, which was disheartening. It was simply a negative screen with weak data." She explained, "Our investment committee, foundation staff, and Imprint were disappointed. I didn't think we were going to go forward." One of the reasons for the unsuccessful first effort by MCM was the lack of knowledge of staff about climate change. This was a new field and a stretch for the team. However, the MCM team recognized it needed to expand its understanding in climate change and took up the challenge. A senior leader explained that once she learned the harm climate change causes globally and the fragility of the planet, she changed her own behavior and has tried to help influence her colleagues at MCM to incorporate climate into their portfolios.

Though at times frustrating, the intentional, iterative, and collaborative process of creating the CES ultimately offered both the investor, McKnight, and its asset managers a product that aligned with mission, used sound metrics and standards for assessing companies' carbon efficiencies, and tracked acceptably well against benchmarks. Moreover, it allowed them to ensure that the ESG expectations of the investor could be met by the asset managers while also meeting the risk return profile McKnight had established for its $200 million investment. The lessons? Meeting the promise while avoiding the perils is not one size fits all. It requires investors to dig in, question, be very clear on what they want, and to push for it. It requires asset managers to have deep knowledge of a topic, capabilities, agility, and commitment to creating impactful ESG products and not merely window dressing. Sending a product to market that doesn't advance agenda to mitigate climate change is a peril. Financial institutions are looking for products to give to their clients. The demand is being felt. Off the shelf products that may not meet client needs are a peril. Having the expertise in-house to avoid problems and "if I had only known" syndrome, is essential.

The outcome? A CES that provides broad equity exposure cost-effectively while assessing, recognizing, and supporting strong climate performance using a combination of screening, rewards, and penalties for climate-related behaviors and proxy voting in support of shareholder resolutions and other corporate initiatives related to climate risk, performance, and disclosure (pfc social impact advisors-Humanity United 2016). The hope was that it would enable investors to send a strong signal of climate change-related action and engagement while maintaining a beta investment profile and managing climate-related investment risk.

Throughout the process, the key stakeholders—MCM, BNY Mellon, and McKnight – exhibited the characteristics of Deliberate Leadership in ways that were true to their organizational cultures.

Conclusion

Bringing the full power of markets to bear on climate change and the myriad of other complex social and environmental challenges facing the planet requires focusing investments for impact. These investments are not just good for our planet, but also make sound financial sense for investors, offering more stable investments that mitigate risk and outperform portfolios that continue to include fossil fuels. Making such investments commonplace requires Deliberate Leadership as demonstrated by the McKnight Foundation—creativity in exploring new solutions, courage to lead and risk failure, and building collaborative relationships with diverse stakeholders and community members based on compassion and candor. Initiatives such as Positive Money are pushing central banks to align their policies with sustainability, while Climate Safe Lending seeks to align European and North American bank lending with the goals of the Paris Climate Accord. The processes, tools, criteria and standards needed to ensure a level playing field for all companies and investors are possible. To get there, however, will take more than better modeling, standards and criteria; it will require leadership deliberately and continually seeking, ready and willing to take risks and adapt, collaborating, keeping communities as the focal point, and compassionately making the hard decisions.

References

1Stock1.com. *Eastman Kodak Company (EKDKQ) Yearly Returns.*

Amel-Zadeh, Amir. 2019. *Mainstreaming Impact.* Oxford Impact Measurement Programme. University of Oxford's Saïd Business School.

Barron, Laignee. 2018. 143 Million People Could Soon Be Displaced Because of Climate Change, World Bank Says. *Time*, March.

Bolinger, Mark, and Joachim Seel. 2018. *Utility-Scale Solar: Empirical Trends in Project Technology, Cost, Performance, and PPA Pricing in the United States—2018 Edition.* The Electricity Markets & Policy Group, Lawrence Berkeley National Laboratory.

Carbon Tracker Initiative. 2011. *Unburnable Carbon—Are the World's Financial Markets Carrying a Carbon Bubble?* July.

Coady, David, Ian Parry, Nghia-Piotr Le, and Baoping Shang. 2019. *Global Fossil Fuel Subsidies Remain Large: An Update Based on Country-Level Estimates.* The International Monetary Fund.

De La Merced, Michael J. 2012. *Eastman Kodak Files for Bankruptcy*, January 19.

DivestInvest. 2018. *Commitments to DivestInvest*. https://www.divestinvest.org/commitments/.

Doyle, Timothy M. 2018. *Ratings That Don't Rate: The Subjective World of ESG Ratings Agencies.* American Council for Capital Formation, July.

Drugmand, Dana. 2019. *Climate Litigation Has Become a Global Trend, New Report Shows.* DeSmog, July.

Eavis, Peter, and Ivan Penn. 2019. California Says PG&E Power Lines Caused Camp Fire That Killed 85. *New York Times*, May.

Egelko, Bob. 2019. *Tesla Fined for Hazardous Waste and Emissions Problems, EPA Says.* San Francisco Chronicle, April 1.

Evan, Will, and Alyssa Jeong Perry. 2018. *Tesla Says Its Factory Is Safer: But It Left Injuries Off the Books.* Center for Investigative Reporting, April 20.

Fernández Campbell, Alexia. 2018. It Took 11 Months to Restore Power to Puerto Rico After Hurricane Maria. A Similar Crisis Could Happen Again. *Vox*, August.

Gara, Antoine, and Joe Deaux. 2013. *Kodak's Bankruptcy: Manufacturing a 21st Century Rebirth.* TheStreet, August,.

Global Fund to End Modern Slavery. *Our Approach.*

Global Sustainable Investment Alliance. 2018. *2018 Global Sustainable Investment Review*. http://www.gsi-alliance.org/trends-report-2018/.

Heath, Alyssa, Melanie Paty, and Will Martindale. 2016. *Global Guide to Responsible Investment Regulation: 2016*. UN Principles for Responsible Investment.

Holder, Michael. 2019. *New Research Finds That ESG Screening Boosts Stock Market Performance*. GreenBiz. Tuesday, January 22.

Huber, Betty M., and Michael Comstock. 2017. *ESG Reports and Ratings: What They Are, Why They Matter*. Harvard Law School Forum on Corporate Governance and Financial Regulation, July 27.

InfluenceMap. 2019. *Climate Funds and Fossil Fuels an Analysis of Climate-Themed Funds Suggests the Need for Oversight of This Emerging Sector*, September.

International Finance Corporation. 2019a. Creating Impact: The Promise of Impact Investing: Appendix B. World Bank Group.

International Finance Corporation. 2019b. Creating Impact: The Promise of Impact Investing. World Bank Group.

International Labor Organization. Undated. *What Is Forced Labour, Modern Slavery and Human Trafficking*.

International Labor Organization. 2018. *World Employment and Social Outlook: Trends 2018*.

Kolodny, Lisa. 2019. *Tesla Shares Soar After Crushing Third-Quarter Earnings*. CNBC, October 23.

Langenbucher, Katja. 2018. *Sustainable Finance and ESG reporting—EU Pushing Ahead, SEC Cautious*. Program on Corporate Compliance and Enforcement New York University School of Law, November 29.

Mackintosh, J. 2018. Is Tesla or Exxon More Sustainable? It Depends Whom you Ask. *Wall Street Journal*. https://on.wsj.com/2MQCC4m, September 17.

Mai, H.J. 2019. *Electricity Costs from Battery Storage Down 76% Since 2012: BNEF*. Utility Dive.

Makower, Joel. 2018. *2018 State of Green Business*. GreenBiz Group and Trucost.

McGrath, Charles. 2019. ESG Interest Driving Data Spending Higher. Pensions and Investments, February 13.

McKibben, Bill. 2012. *Global Warmings Terrifying New Math*. Rolling Stone, July.

Mellon Capital Management. 2014. *Carbon Efficiency Strategy*, September.

Michon, Kathleen. Undated. Tobacco Litigation: History & Recent Developments. NOLO.com.

Minkel, J.R. 2008. *The 2003 Northeast Blackout–Five Years Later*. Scientific American, August.

Mooney, Attracta. 2020. ESG Passes the COVID Challenge. *Financial Times*, June 2.

National Association of State Energy Officials and Energy Futures Initiative. 2018. *2019 U.S. Energy and Employment Report*. https://www.useenergyjobs.org.

Neher, Agnes L. 2017. Stricter European Regulations Favor Sustainable Investments. Sustainable Investment Spotlight—Sustainable Investment Research, Bank J. Safra Sarasin, April 2017.

O'Connor, Casey, and Sarah Labowitz. 2017. *Putting the 'S' in ESG: Measuring Human Rights Performance for Investors*. NYU Stern Center for Business and Human Rights, March.

Pickl, M.J. 2019. The Renewable Energy Strategies of Oil Majors – From Oil to Energy? *Energy Strategy Reviews* 26: 100370. https://doi.org/10.1016/j.esr.2019.100370

pfc social impact advisors. 2016. *Value-Chain Analysis: Partnership for a Carbon Efficiency Strategy*. pfc social impact advisors, April 2016.

pfc social impact advisors. 2018a. *Launching the Working Capital Fund: A Case Study of Humanity United*. pfc social impact advisors, October.

pfc social impact advisors. 2018b. *Investing in Climate Action and Clean Energy Access: Views through a Gender Lens*. pfc social impact advisors, October.

PRI Association and UNEP Finance Initiative. 2011. *Universal Ownership: Why Environmental Externalities Matter to Institutional Investors*.

PRI. 2019. *Principles for Responsible Investment - PRI - Infrastructure Tool Navigator*. Retrieved October 16, 2020 from https://sustainable-infrastructuretools.org/tools/principles-for-responsible-investment-rpi/.

RBC Wealth Management and Bloomberg. 2019. *S&P Dow Jones Indices; Total-Return Data. 5-Year Annualized 2013–2018.*

RE100. Undated. 204 *RE100 Companies Have Made a Commitment to Go '100% Renewable'. Read About the Actions They Are Taking and Why.*

Reznick, Mitch, Michael Viehs, Nachu Chockalingam, Tarandeep Panesar, Gabriela Aguilera Lizarazu, and Julien Moussavi. 2019. *Pricing ESG Risk in Sovereign Credit*. Hermes Investment Management and Beyond Ratings.

Sierra Club. Undated. *Ready for 100: 100% Commitments in Cities, Counties, & States*.

Solar Foundation. 2020. *National Solar Jobs Consensus 2019*. Solar Foundation.

Stevens, Pippa. 2019. *Exxon Mobil Earnings Drop 49% in the third quarter on Lower Oil Prices*. CNBC, November 1.

Sullivan, R., Martindale, W., Feller, E., & Bordon, A. 2019. *Fiduciary Duty in the 21st Century. Geneva, Switzerland: United Nations Global Compact*. Retrieved from https://www.unepfi.org/fileadmin/documents/fiduciary_duty_21st_century.pdf.

Tesla. 2019. *Q3 2019 Update*.

Taylor, A. 2014. Remembering the Exxon Valdez Oil Spill - The Atlantic. *The Atlantic*, p. 1. Retrieved from https://www.theatlantic.com/photo/2014/03/remembering-the-exxon-valdez-oil-spill/100703/, March 24.

The Climate Reality Project. 2016. *Follow the Leader: How 11 Countries Are Shifting to Renewable Energy*, February.

The Corporate ECO Forum and The Nature Conservancy. 2012. *The New Business Imperative: Valuing Natural Capital.*

The McKnight Foundation. 2018. *Audited Financial Statements.*

The McKnight Foundation. 2019. *Why We Invest.*

Thompson, Jennifer. 2018. *Companies with Strong ESG Scores Outperform, Study Finds*. Financial Times Fund Management, August 11.

Tutu, Desmond. 2014. We Need an Apartheid-Style Boycott to Save the Planet. *The Guardian*, April 10.

van Reedt Dortland, Maartje, Dominique Noome, Fred Kruidbos, and Sander Agterhuis. 2019. *Climate Change and Degradation of Natural Resources: Implications for the Military.* Planet Security Initiative, July.

Williams, Cynthia A., and Jill E. Fisch. 2018. *Petition to SEC for Rulemaking on Environmental, Social, and Governance (ESG) Disclosure*, October 1.

Wiser, Ryan, and Mark Bolinger. 2017. *2017 Wind Technologies Market Report.* U.S. Department of Energy's Office of Energy Efficiency and Renewable Energy.

Zhang, Michael. 2017. *This Latest Camera Sales Chart Shows the Compact Camera Near Death*, March.

CHAPTER 4

How Do We Know? Measuring Impact

Ten Lessons About Impact

Understanding positive and negative impact of social investing when tackling Wicked Problems requires investors to discern uncertain, hazardous, and conflicting information. It requires moral judgment, transparency, and intentionality. This chapter begins by sharing key lessons learned intended to guide social investors as they develop strategies for measuring impact. It provides context by highlighting current thinking and best practice from across the field. It explains why now is the right time to scale impact measurement, and the challenges that will involve.

Later in the chapter, Jeremy Nicholls pushes us and the field forward by offering new ways to scale measurement of social value by adapting accounting principles to improve equity, well-being, and sustainability outcomes. However, we begin with ten lessons to keep in mind when developing impact measurement strategies, using Deliberate Leadership as a framework.

Lesson 1: Evaluation and measuring social impact isn't magical, mystifying, or new.

Researchers have been trying to find the causes and solutions of social problems since the 1800s—from the work of social work pioneer Jane Addams who sought to improve the lives of urban poor to James Lind, a doctor of the British Royal Navy who used a design and a control group

G. Peterson et al., *Navigating Big Finance and Big Technology for Global Change*, Palgrave Studies in Impact Finance,
https://doi.org/10.1007/978-3-030-40712-4_4

to find a cure for scurvy by eating citrus fruits. Participatory, community-based evaluation was formally launched in the early 1950s. Business has been assessing financial impact in real time since the invention of capitalism and the bottom line. Evaluation, monitoring, and learning have evolved into a field of professionals across sectors devoting themselves to understanding the numbers and nuance of social change. The American and International Evaluation Association embodies the large global community of strategic learning and is a resource for knowledge and innovation.

Lesson 2: Evaluation and learning is a group sport—learn from, and with, colleagues and avoid reinventing the wheel.

Many colleagues can help a social investor learn and craft a meaningful impact measurement process. Figure 2.3 shared in Chapter 2 shows a network of diverse organizations supporting social change, exemplifying the collaboration that is part of Deliberate Leadership. Each of these organizations spends financial resources on problem-solving and is trying to understand the impact of their investments. They have knowledge to share about their experiences and lessons learned having impact. Swiss Triple Impact initiative, run by B Lab Switzerland, engages Swiss businesses of all sizes and from all sectors to measure their social and environmental impact using B Lab's B Impact Assessment and SDG Action Manager tools, identify concrete opportunities for improvement, and learn from their peers. There are also several global tools that use systems analysis to understand and measure impact including the UN Sustainable Development Goals (SDGs), the Impact Management Project, and the International Finance Corporation's Operating Principles for Impact Management, each of which we describe briefly below.

SDGs and Impact Measures

The SDGs offer the most globally accepted set of major impact goals (Fig. 1.3). The 17 impact goals have 180 specific target goals for 2030, and 245 impact indicators (ranging from 8 to 27 per goal) for determining progress toward those target goals. Table 4.1 shows the diversity of goals, targets and indicators drawing on three of the 17 SDGs.

Table 4.1 Illustration of select SDG goals, targets, and indicators

Goals and targets	*Indicators*
Goal 2. End hunger, achieve food security *and improved nutrition and promote sustainable agriculture*	
2.1 By 2030, end hunger and ensure access by all people, in particular the poor and people in vulnerable situations, including infants, to safe, nutritious and sufficient food all year round	2.1.1 Prevalence of undernourishment 2.1.2 Prevalence of moderate or severe food insecurity in the population, based on the Food Insecurity Experience Scale (FIES) 2.2.2 Prevalence of malnutrition (weight for height $>+2$ or <-2 standard deviation from the median of the WHO Child Growth Standards) among children under 5 years of age, by type (wasting and overweight)
Goal 4. Ensure inclusive and equitable quality education and promote lifelong learning opportunities for all	
4.1 By 2030, ensure that all girls and boys complete free, equitable and quality primary and secondary education leading to relevant and effective learning outcomes	4.1.1 Proportion of children and young people (a) in grades 2/3; (b) at the end of primary; and (c) at the end of lower secondary achieving at least a minimum proficiency level in (i) reading and (ii) mathematics, by sex
4.2 By 2030, ensure that all girls and boys have access to quality early childhood development, care and pre-primary education so that they are ready for primary education	4.2.1 Proportion of children under 5 years of age who are developmentally on track in health, learning and psychosocial well-being, by sex 4.2.2 Participation rate in organized learning (one year before the official primary entry age), by sex
Goal 6. Ensure availability and sustainable management of water and sanitation for all	
6.1 By 2030, achieve universal and equitable access to safe and affordable drinking water for all	6.1.1 Proportion of population using safely managed drinking water services
6.2 By 2030, achieve access to adequate and equitable sanitation and hygiene for all and end open defecation, paying special attention to the needs of women and girls and those in vulnerable situations	6.2.1 Proportion of population using (a) safely managed sanitation services and (b) a hand-washing facility with soap and water

Impact Management Project

The Impact Management Project (IMP) plays a critical role in the social finance field as a convener, facilitator, and consensus builder on measuring, comparing, and reporting social impacts. Created by experts and practitioners, it seeks to build consensus-developed best practice for the field of impact investing and social finance. It intentionally works to ensure its services and products integrate with the SDGs as well as other frameworks. An important recent contribution is its five dimensions of social impact that investors and enterprises need to consider:

- **What** are the outcomes the enterprise is contributing to and how important the outcomes are to stakeholders.
- **Who** (i.e., which stakeholders) are experiencing the outcome and how underserved were they prior to the enterprise's effect.
- **How much** impact is the impact including, how many stakeholders experienced the outcome, what degree of change did they experience, and how long did they experience the outcome for.
- **Contribution** of an enterprise's and/or investor's efforts to outcomes that were likely better than what would have occurred otherwise.
- **Risk** as to the likelihood that impact will be different than expected.

Aligned with best practices of evaluation, this framework offers a thoughtful entry into the types of impacts you should consider in your investing, how you should consider them, and how you should report them.

IFC's Anticipated Impact Measurement and Monitoring System

A third tool for understanding and measuring impact has been developed by the International Finance Corporation (IFC). To help implement its nine Operating Principles for Impact Management (Principles) for its own investing and provide guidance to the 93 signatories of the Principles, IFC has developed its own impact assessment and monitoring framework. Launched in 2017, its Anticipated Impact Measurement and Monitoring (AIMM) system "seeks to give IFC a more rigorous, evidenced-based, end-to-end approach for achieving its triple bottom line" (IFC 2019). From planning and due diligence through implementation and exit, AIMM assesses, monitors, and evaluates each investment across two dimensions—project and market outcomes. Project outcomes include investments' direct effects on stakeholders including neighboring community, and indirect effects on the economy and on society and environment. Its approach has been recognized for its thoughtful, detailed rigor (Chavez 2020; Gabor 2018). Like Iris+, it offers a set of detailed sector-specific frameworks (25 unique sector frameworks) that all follow the same approach.

Together these efforts converge on some basic principles, general ways to approach impact measuring, and some details on what to actually measure. Definitely necessary, the question is whether they are sufficient. The following section explores ways community feedback and feedback learning loops bring the much needed community voice—those beneficiaries of the social, environmental, and hopefully, market impacts—into the impact measurement and management processes.

Lesson 3: Build ground up through community feedback.

> "We should listen to the people we're trying to serve because that's ethical and moral, and in a philosophical sense they are the ones who should be the ultimate arbiters of what it takes to make their lives better, and whether their lives are getting better."
>
> Dennis Whittle

It should be common sense that communities being served by social investment should be at the center of impact measurement. Yet, often they are last to be consulted about either the support and services they need or whether the funded program had a positive or negative impact on their lives. Dennis Whittle calls community feedback, "the smart and right thing to do" (Sarkisova 2016). "Smart" because resources can be best used when target effectively and "right" because it is ethical to have people be the ultimate arbiters of what they need to make their lives better.

There are many ways to build the communities that can apply pressure for change. One example is the ourEconomy media hub run by openDemocracy. openDemocracy uses its media platform as part of an effort to disrupt and challenge prevailing economic orthodoxies in the media; communicate the growing consensus around a new economic paradigm to a wider global audience; influence public opinion and the policy debate;

and accelerate the transition to a fairer and more sustainable economy. Similarly, the Economic Change Unit seeks to amplify efforts to realize a more sustainable, just and resilient economy by providing critical functions in communications, network-building and strategic coordination that will enhance and amplify aligned efforts within the economic systems change movement, particularly within the United Kingdom.

Lesson 4: Community engagement is not a new concept.

Consumer-facing companies have long tried to nurture communities so that they can promote and test their products, and position themselves as brands that are part of people's everyday lives. But if the concept of community engagement, today consumer-driven communities have reached levels that were impossible to manage in the past. It is estimated that there are over 5.5 billion Google searches per day in 2020 or an estimated 63,000 search queries done per second (Ardor SEO 2020). The world is awash with constant, instant data and feedback. Opinions are shared widely and on-demand, when flights are delayed, or restaurant service is poor. Thoughts, ideas, and even lifestyle choices on social media are shared in a nanosecond. With the proliferation of high-speed internet and low-cost mobile devices, the classic business mantra that "the customer is always right" has evolved into the far more demanding notion of "customer-centricity," where products and services are built to be tailored to varying, individual needs. Whether they like it or not, companies have come to embrace customer feedback and the most successful among them, such as Amazon and Facebook, have used it to build market dominance.

Lesson 5: Community feedback and the glass ceiling.

Yet, as Walmart collects over 2.5 petabytes of customer data per hour (and globally, the company processes about $36 Million an hour in sales each day) (Gunelius 2014), Fay Twersky, Vice President, William and Flora Hewlett Foundation (Hewlett Foundation) points out that community voices "haven't yet broken though the glass ceiling of philanthropy" (Twersky et al. 2013). This is not to suggest that big data and customer relationships are without significant failings in the business world, or that they are always transferable or appropriate for the social sector, but the social finance and social service community (the social sector) have not embraced fully the norm of seeking out and adapting to user feedback with quite the same fervor as a variety of other disciplines, ranging from social work and design thinking to manufacturing and politics.

According to a survey of US nonprofits by the Center for Effective Philanthropy, 37% collect and use "beneficiary" feedback during the planning, implementation, and reflection phases of their programs, and most believe that foundation funders "lack a deep understanding of their intended beneficiaries' needs" (Buteau et al. 2014). This suggests an underappreciation for listening to community feedback, to say nothing of the quality or authenticity of this feedback, or the social sector's propensity to learn and share from it.

Lesson 6: Overcome the Excuses.

As Twersky explains that for many in the philanthropy world, "Feedback takes too much time; it feels uncomfortable; it is another thing to do," and while customers drive revenues in the for-profit sector, money flows top-down in the nonprofit world, leaving little direct incentive for funders and grantees to listen to community.

To address this field-wide shortcoming, Twersky co-founded Fund for Shared Insight and Listen4Good to help the field of philanthropy support innovative ways to institutionalize its commitment to community voice and feedback. More than 100 social investors are members of these two affiliated groups to support the practice of community listening and feedback. Hewlett supported a case study, *The Power of Feedback: Solving Wicked Problems through Listening and Learning* (pfc 2017) to help social investors find ways to integrate community feedback loop into their investment strategy. Our final four lessons are ones taken from that study.

Lesson 7: Feedback should be integrated with an overall learning strategy.

Twersky believes that feedback is one of three legs of a stool for creating well-rounded learning organizations: "*Monitoring* allows for pulse taking; *evaluation* provides independent rigor on determining whether outcomes were achieved; and *feedback loops* allow for real-time learning and innovation."

Lesson 8: A commitment of leadership is essential for a successful impact measurement strategy.

Our team believes that Twersky's three-legged stool needs either a fourth leg or a seat to create stability. Leadership within the investor organization and beneficiary make the commitment to learning to be successful. Accepting challenges when confronted with complex challenges often requires changing behavior in organizational culture and expectations. Without committed leadership, systemic learning may not happen. Kathy Reich, co-chair of Fund for Shared Insight and the Director of the Ford Foundation's Building Institutions and Networks (BUILD) initiative, adds that learning, listening, and reflecting must be part of the DNA of organizations—and for many organizations, they simply aren't: "Culture change is really hard," she says, "It's one of the toughest things that you can do."

Lesson 9: Power and fear are obstacles to feedback.

Social investors have the power to control resources. Unless there is a culture of trust and candor, investees are fearful of sharing negative experiences, even if they can ultimately improve performance. This issue is tied to power dynamics, the fear of failure and preoccupation with success at the investor level trickles down to the investee and community level where it gets reinforced. This can be described as a "doom loop" that can dog organizations when they are faced with failure and are afraid to report negative community feedback to funders.

Lesson 10: Examine examples of feedback models.

More honest, useful feedback can be acquired in a number of ways. Feedback Lab, for instance, uses a five-step approach illustrated in the diagram below to incorporate community feedback: design, collect, analyze, dialogue, and course correct (Fig. 4.1).

Concern Worldwide (Concern) is a 50-year old international humanitarian organization that offers great examples of how deep community feedback mechanisms are central to success. Its 3500 member staff and consultants work in 24 of the most fragile countries challenged by deep Wicked Problems—war, natural disaster, violence, poverty, and profound gender inequality (Concern 2018). Its work in Kenya and Pakistan illustrate its approach.

Since 2002, Concern has worked in Kenya predominantly with vulnerable communities living in rural, arid, and semi-arid lands in the north and informal settlements in Nairobi. Its work is driven by its Community Conversations (CC) project. CC is a participatory, socially transformative approach that empowers communities to analyze complex social-economic and cultural issues associated with low community development, ultimately producing behavioral change within vulnerable communities. It is a facilitated community dialogue where members of the community come together to discuss the causes of underdevelopment, arrive at potential resolutions, and plan for and implement actions to change their circumstances (Fig. 4.2). The process in Kenya addresses the underlying causes of health concerns by creating a space for relationship

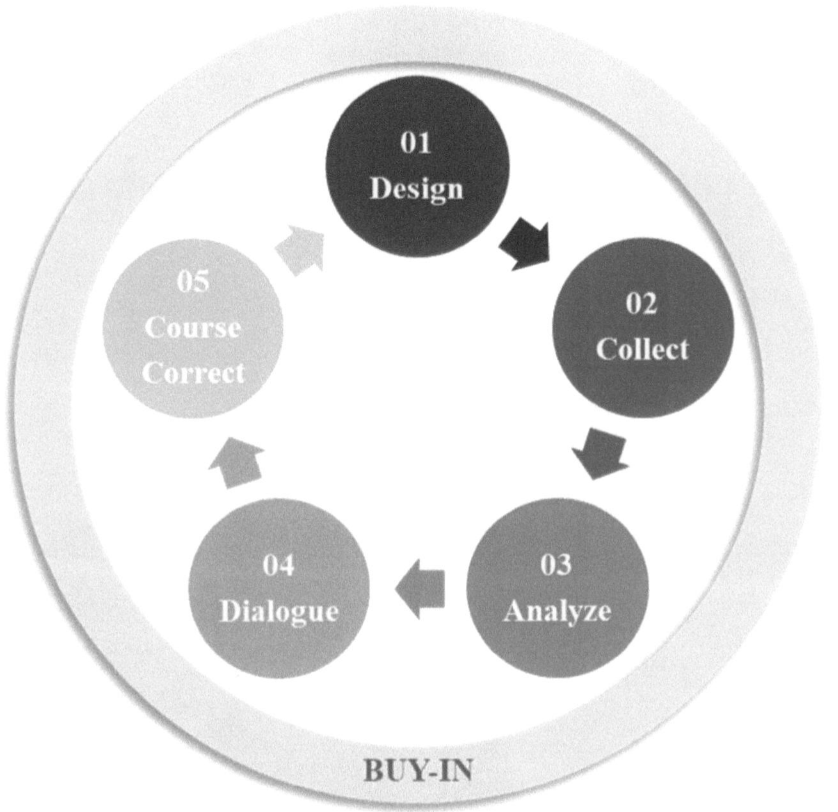

Fig. 4.1 The feedback loop (*Source* Adapted from Feedback Labs, 2017)

building; analyzing and gathering community data and context; deepening community dialogue; emphasizing community decision-making and action; and reflecting and learning together.

Like Feedback Lab and in keeping with Deliberate Leadership, it is an iterative process engaging the community in codesign, data collection and analysis, and reflection and adaptation. Working with and for the community helps prevent harm and maximizes positive impact.

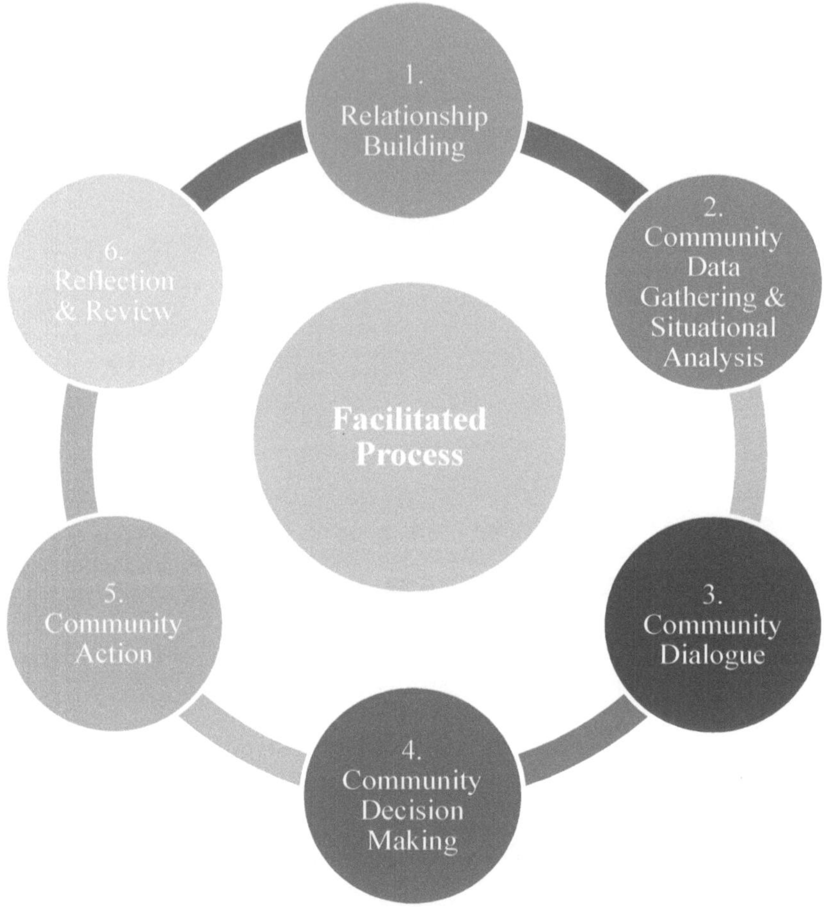

Fig. 4.2 Concern's community conversations methodology (*Source:* Developed from Concern Worldwide Community Conversations Trainer of Trainers Manual, 2013)

Time to Scale Impact Measurement

Jeremy Nicholls has been doing evaluation for several decades. As a co-founder of Social Value International, he and his team have taught best practice to social investors globally. Jeremy's thinking on the best way to scale community-based and integrate Deliberate Leadership into the ethos of an organization's learning approach is to build on practices honed through accounting practices relating to materiality.

The more than $200 trillion under investment isn't static. It marches to the tune of increasing returns informed by reported profits. As we have discussed in Chapter 3, investment decisions will increasingly need to be informed by information on social and environmental impact, and so we need to change the tune. Investment must be underpinned by a system of impact accounting in order to facilitate continuing, and increasing, investment for organizations doing good, to ensure transparency for investors and accountability for the people and communities affected by Wicked Problems and the efforts to address them.

This chapter continues with the basis of financial accounting, and how this system can serve as a model for impact accounting that facilitates comparison and decisions that ultimately increase impact and ultimately to fundamental change in how society accounts for value. To do so, impact accounting must come to shared answers to the questions of why measure, who measures, what to measure, and how to measure it? Drawing on examples from the United Kingdom, financial accounting also serves as a model for standardization of terms, metrics and reporting. While financial accounting has contributed to many of the Wicked Problems impact investing aspires to solve (e.g. the social and environmental consequences of externalizing company behavior), a common basis for financial and impact accounting will facilitate the integration of impact to transform the ways we assess value, returns and externalities, and ensuring the broader consideration and valuing of social and economic impacts beyond impact investing.

To develop a common approach to creating value that takes account of economic, social and environmental worth in allocating resources, we need to understand how our increasingly global approach to understanding financial value developed. There is much to celebrate in this approach. It is global, socially constructed, and yet good enough to support investment decisions which have contributed to increases in global GDP. The key to successfully integrating the triple bottom line of people, planet, and profits lies in the building blocks of financial accounting. Before we journey into those foundational pieces, we first need to discuss the issue of impact—how we define it and whose benefit is to be considered.

The Challenge for Impact

While there is a growing convergence on what we mean by impact, not all impacts are equal and not all are universally accepted. We may all be keen on empowerment until we realize it's a relative measure; if I have more power, you have less. Whoever is at risk of having less power is going to cling to it and argue for ways of defining "impact" and "more" in ways that don't change anything too fundamental.

If financial investments are moving to new opportunities, this is all about the allocation of scarce resources, politics, and power. Impact can be seen as a response to the world's Wicked Problems, but it can also be seen as a response to saturated markets and declining long-term returns, where investors search out new opportunities for return and enterprises seek to differentiate and compete based on their sustainability or impact performance. We run the risk of creating an industry around impact that, in the end, may mean slightly different types of investment, but doesn't actually change anything fundamental about the allocation of resources, power and quality of life.

Just in case there is any doubt, we do need to change something fundamental. Even without the COVID-19 pandemic, the global economy was suffering a crisis—climate change and widening inequality threaten the lives of billions on lower incomes, increasingly the lives and stability of the middle classes, and certainly the lives of future generations. The global economy is not designed to stop this happening. Only by embedding the consideration of social and environmental outcomes alongside financial outcomes when making decisions about the allocation of resources will we be able to change the basis of our global economy.

Impact investing offers such considerations. But it also could reinforce inequality if the existing order of power and wealth does not change (Foxworth 2018). We need a fundamental change in how resources are allocated, and this will have implications for how impact is defined, measured, and managed.

The Current Economic System, Climate Change, and Inequality

Since investment already has a way of measuring performance—financial accounting—it is useful to see how this system developed as the basis for decisions to increase financial value. This will provide useful insights into what we need in order to successfully measure and increase "impact." If decisions are going to take both impact and financial value into account, there also needs to be some read across between the two.

After all, in terms of financial value, our financial system has been incredibly effective, playing its part in increasing GDP (see Fig. 4.3). A system that unleashed an equivalent amount of "impact," alongside financial value, will surely address our current challenges.

Our financial system has been successful in supporting a general increase in wealth. Alongside it, however, is increasing financial inequality and degradation of the natural resources, including advancing climate change. Just before the 2008 financial crisis, an Oxfam report noted that 82% of wealth created worldwide was going to the top 1%. "The poorest half saw no increase at all. All over the world, the economy of the 1% is built on the backs of low paid workers, often women, who are paid poverty wages and denied basic rights" (Oxfam 2018). That situation did not improve in the wake of the crisis, and it took a decade or longer for the incomes of the many to return to pre-financial crisis levels. As the well-known "elephant graph" shows (Fig. 4.4), the increasing wealth of the middle classes in India and China meant that not all growth has been captured by the richest 1%. But a lot of it—27%—has. Moreover, the growth of the middle classes in emerging economies has flattened out

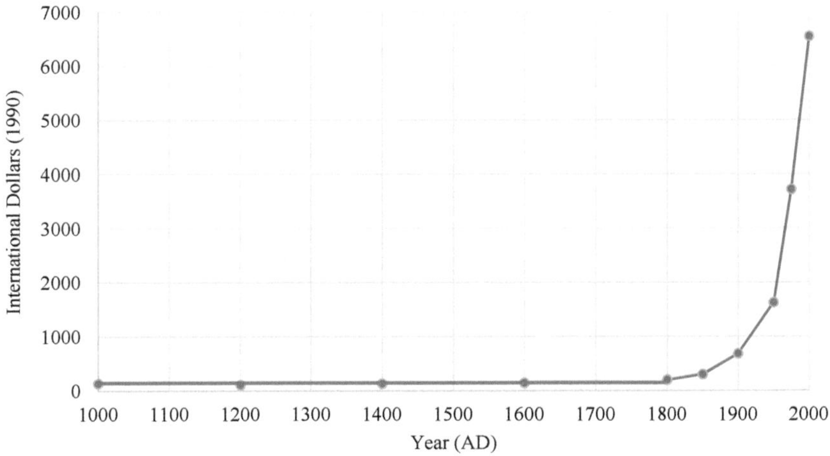

Fig. 4.3 Estimates of average world GDP per capita (*Source* Adapted from Bradford De Long 1998)

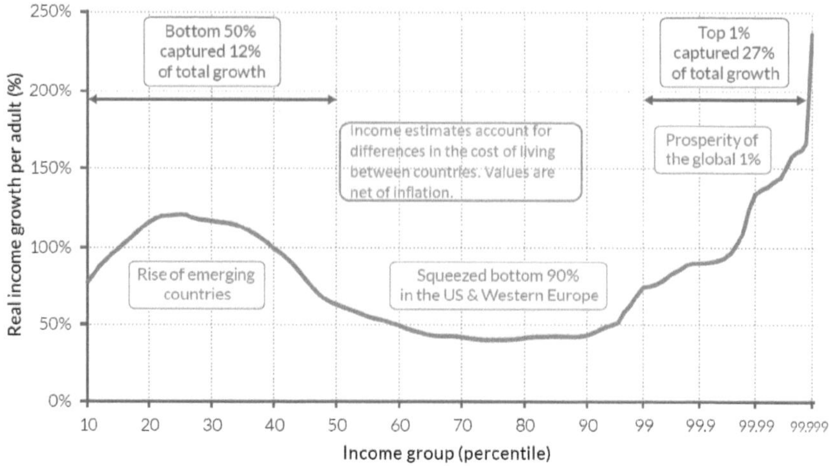

Fig. 4.4 The elephant curve of global inequality and growth, 1980–2016 (*Source* Adapted from Alvaredo et al. World Inequality Report 2018)

over the last five years. And that was without taking into consideration the economic consequences of COVID-19. If this trend continues this will become a "cobra curve."

The reported success in reducing inequality is also based on the proportion of people in poverty. Although the proportion of people in extreme poverty (under $1.90 per day) has declined, it is debatable whether the absolute number, around 800 million, has changed much since 1800. And there are now several billion people on low incomes between $1.90 and $10 per day.

Recognition that this is a problem extends beyond academic critiques (for example from Stiglitz et al. 2018); mainstream finance organizations like the International Monetary Fund (IMF) and Organization for Economic Cooperation and Development (OECD) have published work on inequality and growth. A growing number of business initiatives reference inequality, including the Coalition for Inclusive Capitalism and the Social and Human Capital Coalition. As noted in the first chapter, the UN's SDGs include a specific goal to reduce inequality in addition to a goal to end poverty. Governments support policies for inclusive growth and poverty reduction. Yet, despite these interventions, wealth inequality has continued to increase.

At the same time, global efforts to reduce carbon emissions have had mixed success. Despite some international agreements and targets, as well as national policies, carbon levels continue to increase, now standing at over 414 parts per million (Scripps 2019), with the UK's Metoffice predicting a further increase of 2.75 ppm in 2019 (United Kingdom National Meteorological Service 2019). Although predictions of increases in temperature from further increases in carbon are difficult, levels of over 500 ppm are likely to mean the temperature increase would exceed the international consensus goal of keeping the global average temperature to below 2 °C above pre-industrial levels (Gao et al. 2017).

This is the context for impact, whether as part of impact investing or any other activity. The test is whether impact investing contributes to reducing both inequality and the rate of climate change.

Capturing Economic, Social, and Environmental Value

The above examples show that economic value alone is insufficient to capture the full range of meaningful impact organizations such as businesses can have. Society has recognized that defining economic value solely in financial terms has left out other significant sources of value—environmental and social—often resulting in them being negatively affected. This has given rise to a critique of GDP as an inaccurate measure of development, and a number of proposals to either supplement or replace it, for example the social progress index (2019 Social Progress Index 2019) and approaches to measuring happiness (Helliwell et al. 2019). It also gave rise to sustainability reporting, cost–benefit analysis, and impact measurement, all addressing social and environmental outcomes and supplementing economic value.

At the same time, our approach to what we mean by "economic" has been driven by our international economic system rather than by the science of economics. Definitions of economics include the study of production, consumption, and distribution, all of which have social and environmental consequences. For the economic system, economics has too often come to mean financial; and social and environmental issues have been treated as externalities. Yet, treating these issues as externalities downplays their relevance and significance to the economy.

The cause of this separation dates back to before the start of economics. Although there are two main international legal systems, common and civil, the influence of common law on approaches to economics, and social and environmental sustainability, is important.

Our current economic system and much economic theory starts with contract law, and financial reporting focuses on the performance of a businesses' contracts: of purchase and sale; of employment; as well as legal liabilities for taxes. In pursuing its legal contracts there may be consequences for contracted people, but also, through equity law, for people with whom there is no contract. Economics considered these to be externalities, a language rooted in the separation between common law and equity law. Impact often addresses externalities, both intended and unintended. If financial value refers to the performance resulting from contracts, then impact can be thought of as referring to the performance of issues that relate to equity, to externalities. Although law has since become more integrated, economics and the understanding of value has retained this separation.

Financial Value and Financial Accounting

Financial value is determined by an accounting process approximating the value being created or lost by those involved. This process is predominantly driven by the idea that the amount people pay for goods or services represents the value those goods or services hold for them. In a complex supply chain, this is an imprecise estimate that has real consequences on access to resources.

Financial accounting has been around for a long time, dating back as early as the twelfth century (Smith 2018). In its current form it arose from the development of the limited liability company in the nineteenth century. The current approach to accounting can be explored through some basic questions that any accounting process will address: Why measure? Who measures? What do we measure? How do we measure?

Why Measure?

Financial accounting measures financial value for the people who are investing so they can make decisions on whether to buy, sell, or hold their investments, most commonly so that they can increase the financial value they receive from their investments. In practice this has led to behavior, especially in investment managers who have a duty to act in the interests of their clients (i.e., the underlying asset owners), that seeks to increase financial returns over the short to medium term. The decision of what to measure is then those things that would matter to help people make decisions to "increase their financial returns." If information doesn't help choose between investments' ability to generate financial value, then it doesn't matter.

The purpose of this measurement is not to measure the financial value per se, but to assess performance. Accounting is the way in which investors (and governments in relation to tax) hold businesses accountable and the drive for business to respond to their investors' objectives is relentless. The question of how to measure is not just about a series of techniques, but also how well to measure, and how accurate the measurement needs to be to inform these decisions.

Investors are aware that there are risks in any investment and expected returns are risk-adjusted. Financial accounting seeks to minimize the risk that the accounts are incomplete or inaccurate. It does not address the risk of expected future returns which relate to the underlying business model, future markets, the management team, etc. Financial accounting is generally considered a record of past performance but in making investments and choosing between options an investor has to assess both financial projections and risk, and seek other information alongside any financial accounts and projections to assess this risk. For public listings where profit forecasts are included, they will be examined by the reporting accountants or auditors in accordance with established standards. This forms only a small part of the requirements for public offers, the complexity of which is explored, for example, in "Initial Public Offers: A guide to the UK listing regime" (Clifford Chance 2018). As limited liability and the development of secondary markets for shares has increased alongside the scale of investment, there has been a drive to protect investors and to standardize accounts to address the needs of large numbers of investors who rarely know the people running the enterprises in which they invest.

The recognition of risk has created a secondary market for insuring against risk (for example, derivatives), and a risk-based approach to portfolio management, balancing riskier investments with potential higher returns with safer investments with lower returns.

Measurement is designed to assess performance: organizations can be held to account for that performance and investors can move their investments where they are not satisfied with performance. As a stakeholder there is a feedback loop that drives performance.

Who Measures?

Clearly, it's the organization that has received the investment that is going to prepare the accounts. When managers' ability to increase salaries or keep their jobs is dependent on maintaining and increasing investment in the business, there is a conflict of interest. Consequently, accounts are checked, or audited, by a third party acting on behalf of investors (even if they are paid by the organization).

What Is Measured?

The UK Companies Act requires accounts to be prepared that are **true and fair.** Although what this is has not been legally defined, Section 393 of the Act states: "(a) in the case of the balance sheet, give a true and fair view of the state of affairs of the company as at the end of the financial year, and, (b) in the case of the profit and loss account, give a true and fair view of the profit or loss of the company for the financial year." Meanwhile, Section 395 states: "(1) A company's individual accounts may be prepared—(a) in accordance with section 396 ('Companies Act individual accounts'), or (b) in accordance with international accounting standards ('IAS individual accounts')."

This would suggest that "true and fair" can mean what is in accordance with international standards, although the Financial Reporting Council (FRC) has released separate guidance that allows true and fair considerations to override international accounting standards (Financial Reporting Council 2014). International standards are designed to ensure that financial statements are free from material misstatements and faithfully represent the financial performance and position of the entity.

True and fair are both heavily laden words given the degree of judgment necessary in preparing accounts, and especially in determining what should be included or excluded. Given the level of subjective judgment required, it is of course difficult to see how accounts can be "true" in the sense of being in accordance with fact and objective reality. Accounts are expected to reflect economic reality though (Financial Reporting Council 2014). Economic reality is not defined, and the current legal debates over, for example, when or whether people are employed by a business or are self-employed, shows why this is not easy to define.

If economics are generally defined as studies of the production, consumption, and distribution of goods and services, then accounts would need to reflect all three; yet accounts do not provide much, if any, information on distribution. In practice, economic decisions quickly become interpreted as restricted to financial decisions, specifically to decisions to increase financial returns and the wealth of individual investors. This is the basis for financial accounting, to provide current and future investors with information to make decisions to buy, sell, or hold investments in order to increase financial returns.

In reality there are many investors, with many different motivations (even if we limit the definition of economic to the financial) and different requirements for risk and return. They may have an even greater range of difference among their motivations if economic value including distribution. It would not be possible to produce different accounts reflecting the different information that each investor requires. We have to standardize, and we have standardized around an *assumed* individual only interested in financial returns.

In addition, the scope of accounting is limited to those things that matter that are the responsibility of the reporting organization within the accounting period. This is not limited to contracts, although contracts to buy and sell services are generally the starting point. There will be other legally enforceable liabilities such as taxes. There may be quasi-contracts where the law has imposed liability independent of an agreement between those involved. There can also be provisions which have not yet been legally imposed, but where they are probable the value should be included in the calculation of profit. If not probable, or if reliable measurement is not possible, they are included as a note to the accounts as a contingent liability (and of course a standard, IAS 37, that provides guidance).

How to Measure?

How should this all be measured? Measurement needs to be good enough to allow investors to make these decisions, decisions that will generally involve a comparison with a forecast. The question of whether selling one investment and buying another leads to higher returns is a prediction, an informed guess. Accounting information should be good enough for this purpose and not for any other. Good enough requires measurement to be consistent, to compare performance against past results, to compare different businesses, and against expected future performance.

There are then two further questions.

How do we decide what should be included in accounts in practice? This is not only the question of what matters, but also the question of when things that matter should be recognized. For example, when does a sale become included in a business' income statement? Revenue recognition is a complex area and there is a separate standard, IFRS 15 (IFRS Foundation), dedicated to the question. Liability recognition is relatively easy for legally binding contracts, but where the business may have incurred liability, for example as a result of fraud, liabilities will be more difficult to identify and depend on the control environment.

How do we value what has been included? Again, this might be simple enough for cash transactions reflecting market prices, but there are many other resources available to a business that underpin its ability to create financial value and therefore matter to our investors. There is the assumption here that market prices represent the "true" value. The fact that the value of an extra dollar is lower to a rich person than it is to a poor person, or that negotiating power between those involved in contracts is rarely equal, is not addressed.

There is a standard on Fair Value Measurement, IFRS 13, to provide guidance in the absence of market prices. IFRS 13 states that when measuring fair value, the objective is to estimate the price at which an orderly transaction to sell an asset or to transfer a liability **would** take place between market participants at the measurement date under **current** market conditions (i.e., to estimate an exit price).

Most importantly, accounting practice and accounting standards have developed to address these questions and provide guidance to preparers and auditors of accounts. These are necessary but not sufficient requirements for an effective ecosystem.

The Wider Ecosystem

Financial accounting sits within a wider ecosystem that is designed to support individuals in creating financial value. The need for audit has already been raised and is a fundamental protection for investors giving their money to third parties and receiving reports from them. Secondary markets have developed to support investors with different skills and different risk appetites, complete with analysts, investment managers, and financial advisors. Customers provide feedback all the time in different ways.

Critically, there is extensive regulation. Contract law underpins the system. In the United Kingdom the Companies Act sets out the duties of directors and the requirement to produce accounts, the standard to which they should be prepared, and the need for audit. Directors have extensive duties, including to act within powers; to promote the success of the company; to exercise independent judgment; to exercise reasonable care, skill, and diligence; and to avoid conflicts of interest. Advisors and other intermediaries are regulated and supported by professional bodies. There are separate bodies to oversee the system, like the FRC. Finally, there is an active and free press that reports on all aspects of the ecosystem, good and bad. The system is expensive but necessary to support the levels of ongoing investment that underpin our economies.

All this means that there are consequences. Organization that do not perform in line with expectations, whose accounts are not materially accurate, or who break the law will face consequences. Staff may lose their jobs, the cost of capital may increase, and ultimately the organization may have to close.

The financial accounting ecosystem is not value-free or distribution-neutral. Simply because it is not interested in distribution and equity issues does not mean that the system has no effect on distribution. In fact, by limiting itself to a narrow definition of economic, financial accounting contributes to widening inequality and climate change. Financial opportunities and returns are not equally distributed. In any period, by chance, some people will do better than others. In the next period some of them will do better again. Inequality will arise by chance. In reality this will be reinforced by unequal access to opportunities and the actions that people can take to maintain their position.

What Are the Lessons for Impact Investing?

The consequence of financial accounting has been to focus on individual wealth-maximizing behavior without accountability for the global consequences. The nascent impact field presents an opportunity to develop a method of accounting that incorporates the values of Deliberate Leadership: creativity to imagine new approaches to an established practice; collecting the data required for courageous accountability and compassionate decisions that lead to more impact; building collaborative community that brings along the existing financial accounting ecosystem—and its capital—to incorporate social and environmental returns; and candor in acknowledging risks and managing any perverse incentives.

If there is to be a holistic approach to accounting for value, then we need to be able to account for the missing value, or at least as much of it as possible. Impact accounting will need to underpin impact investing in the same ways financial accounting underpins financial investment. It will need to assess performance in creating positive impact and include effective feedback loops to those experiencing the impact with consequences for poor performance. The approach that financial accounting took to answering the questions in this section will be useful in developing impact accounting, especially as integrating the two approaches will mean that they need to be comparable and consistent. Moreover:

- The approach we take to understanding what we mean by impact will not be value-free or distribution-neutral but has to empower those experiencing impact
- Financial accounting contributes to the Wicked Problems impact investing is seeking to address and yet will need to be used alongside approaches to understand and manage impact.
- The basis of financial accounting needs to be updated, but the principle that impact accounting needs to start with a single user with a single purpose will be necessary for consistency.

The State of Impact: What Do We Mean by More Impact?

As noted in the previous chapter on ESGs, investing for social and environmental impact is a growing field. Not all impacts are equal, it's nothing like as common as financial accounting, and impact reports remain the exception rather than the rule. The approaches to accounting for impact remain varied in practice, and the extent to which decisions are being made based on impact data is uncertain. However, to get a better idea of where thinking and practice to do with impact accounting stands today, let us ask some of the same questions we posed in relation to financial accounting. Questions about why, who, what, and how helped explain how financial accounting has taken the directions it has, and why it has limitations when we want to understand value in a broader sense. Now we ask those same questions again, but with a focus on social and environmental impact as well. We will also look at the institutional ecosystem to support impact accounting because we have seen that one of the reasons financial accounting has become so dominant is because of the strength of the institutions that support it. Finally, we will ask what needs to be done if the new types of accounting and impact measurement are to become as strong as those focused on financial value.

Why Measure Social and Environmental Impact?

The purpose of measurement would seem to be so that we can make decisions that increase positive impact and reduce negative impact and at an effective rate However, there are other related reasons to measure impact, including accountability, legitimacy, and marketing, though all these would benefit from increasing impact. So, the purpose of measurement could be to choose options for allocating resources that have a more positive impact. Like financial accounting, the focus will be on decision-making, but unlike financial accounting, where there is clarity on what is meant by finance, the same is not true for impact.

Impact is all the rage, but it is not often clear what it means. *A Guide to the Impact Revolution* (Cohen 2018) defines impact as "the potential of an action to improve lives and the planet," while, for Social Value International, impact relates to social value, "the quantification of the relative importance that people place on the changes they experience in their lives." One focuses on people, the other on people and planet. Both recognize the importance of increasing impact, although the focus on improvement risks failing to account for changes that make things worse. The Future-Fit Foundation's Business Benchmark tries to address this through its "break-even goals." (See Case Study in Chapter 6.) The Business Benchmark is rooted in the social and environmental systems conditions that a body of scientists argue are the minimum requirements for a sustainable, regenerative planet. The break-even goals are the bare minimum an organization needs to achieve in order that its actions do not breach those systems conditions. By using a common set of systems conditions that can be applied to any organization or industry, and by defining the minimum that is needed to avoid social and/or environmental degeneration, the Business Benchmark provides a holistic and consistent vision for demonstrating impact

The fundamental lack of consistency that is typical of much of the ESG and sustainability space will inevitably produce different measures of impact that cannot be easily used for making comparisons and therefore decisions to allocate resources between organizations to create more impact. We saw an example of this in Chapter 3 when we compared the very different valuations of Tesla and ExxonMobil that were made depending on what ESG indicators were used. Organizations that measure impact within their own operations can make internal comparisons, but the degree of impact will depend on what is chosen. For example, excluding negative impacts from what is measured means that a decision to move resources to do something with an expected higher positive impact could have a larger, but ignored, negative impact. Overall, it would reduce impact and yet still be selected. Avoiding this risk inevitably leads to an approach to impact accounting that considers all impacts, positive and negative. However, like financial accounting, it is neither possible nor necessary to account for every impact, only the ones that matter need to be included. So, like finance, impact accounting will need to determine materiality.

Focusing on the question of more impact means making comparisons of relative importance. There are different perspectives about how to account for changes to the planet, environment, and ecosystem compared to changes to people's lives. Some argue that these changes result in changes to people's lives, both current and future generations, and that therefore a focus on changes in peoples' lives will address changes to the planet. Others argue that they should be considered separately. While both people and our planet have intrinsic value, the focus is on whether one course of action has a more positive impact than another. Somewhere in this comparison, people's perception of relative importance will be inescapable.

As these issues are resolved, more options can be compared, and more decisions made to increase net impact. The focus is still on obtaining good enough data to make that comparison and choose an option, remembering that these are based at least in part on forecasts of the future.

In finance, the driver is investors and their choices between investments. This, and the ecosystem that supports it, effectively forces organizations to constantly choose how they allocate resources, and redesign existing products and services to increase financial value. A well-established ecosystem doesn't exist for social and environmental values and impact; there is as yet no consistency in what and how people measure (or even identify what should be measured) in practice. Organizations seeking investments, or to enhance their brand, or to better understand the "external" risks, can still make comparisons based on their own standardized approaches even if these approaches are not shared. The people investing in impact could assess performance based on the frequency at which options are generated, considered, and implemented, but they may not be able to assess performance based on the impact generated.

We discussed standardization in Chapter 3, noting that although there are various initiatives to move in that direction, it is a long way from the uniformity and cross-organization transferability that exists for financial accounting. It is also a long way from valuing impact rather than just performance. If the drive for standardization of measurement and reporting so that investors can make comparisons ignores this, then organizations run the risk of creating less impact than they could with the same resources. In addition, there is a risk that standardization for investors is not based on data that is useful for organizations to make comparisons and is therefore not useful for anything other than reporting. Any standardization should be based on data that is necessary and useful for comparing options for increasing impact. External pressure should first encourage data use and second encourage consistency in what is necessary for data to be useful.

Who Are We Measuring for?

A quick answer might be the investors. However, if the impact is being received by people then the measurement is really for the people experiencing the changes to their lives. This is analogous to financial accounting which is for the people who receive the financial returns. Impact accounting is for the people who get the social returns.

But there is a disconnect now. Financial accounting measures so that the people getting the financial returns can make decisions about those financial returns. Impact accounting measures so that the people receiving the change in their lives can make decisions about the changes in their lives—only they can't, or at least not to the same extent as financial investors. Impact investing addresses issues of equity and distribution, where the populations of intended impact have less power or are relatively underserved. In neither case are they as able to make decisions and, critically, are, by definition, less able to hold organizations accountable than investors are in relation to financial returns.

Alternatively, we could say impact accounting measures so that investors can make decisions about the change in other people's lives. Either way there is a breakdown between principal and agent. Investors are making decisions on behalf of the people getting the impact and are acting in their interest. This would mean that the people receiving the impact are the principal and the investor is their agent (Fig. 4.5). The investor could be argued to have a fiduciary duty to those that receive the impact. This would bring impact into the realm of common law and it would no longer be an externality.

Traditionally the responsibility for the impact is seen as resting with the organization creating the impact. In this case it would now be indirect, and the primary responsibility would rest with the investor. While we are measuring for the people who get the impact, the organization collecting the data will be reporting to the investor so that the investor can fulfill their responsibility to the people who get the impact.

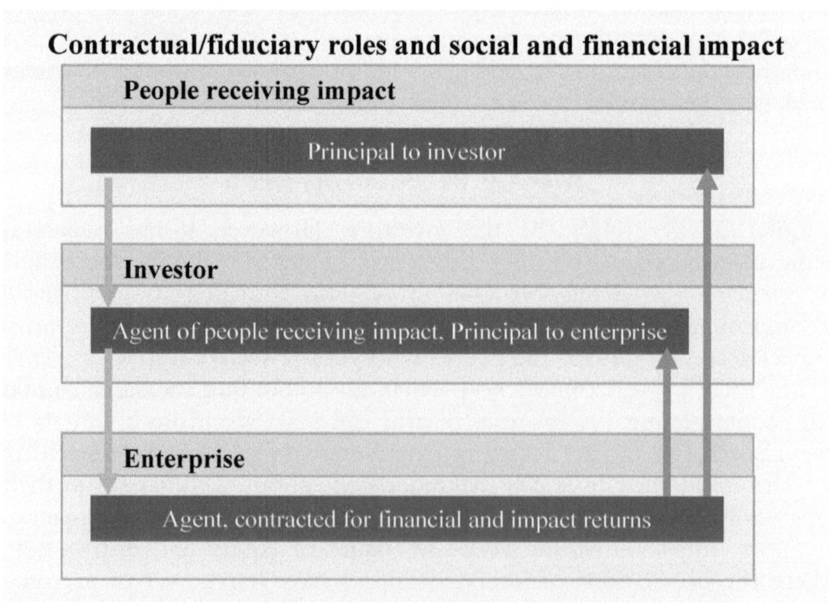

Fig. 4.5 Investors' agency and fiduciary duty to whom?

The consequence of this current gap in accountability is that there is no relentless pressure to increase impact in the same way there is for financial value, and reported impact is likely to be lower than it could be. There is also less pressure for standardization. Although the fact that the majority of people (whose lives are changing) rarely know the managers of the enterprises (that are creating that change) should drive standardization, the breakdown between principal and agent stops this from happening.

Better perhaps would be to say that impact accounting measures **as if** the people experiencing the change in their lives could make decisions about the change in their lives, and **as if** they could hold the organization to account. This won't be enough to ensure that the data is used but it should lead to the data that will be the minimum necessary. As already noted in the case of the Future-Fit Foundation's Business Benchmark, a rounded understanding of how an organization impacts on the different elements of a regenerative social and environmental system is important so that organizations do not pick and choose what areas they want to be held accountable for.

Focusing on those getting the impact also provides an insight into what is meant by impact. While impact will be a change, it is likely to be a change in things that matter to people, a change in their well-being. Well-being can be defined as a balanced state where no fundamental psychological or physical human needs are significantly deficient, and the foundations of physical and psychological health are present in enough measure to meet challenges faced. It is also referred to as a state of flourishing or a "good life" and exists at individual, household, country and global level. This definition incorporates people's sense of self-worth and this would include addressing inequality.

Choosing the Option with a "Better" Impact

As with financial investments, investment that took impact into account will inevitably require a choice between different mixes of return and impact. These choices are generally informed by the investor's personal subjectivity of the relative importance of the impact.

There will be trade-offs in the impact, between long term and short term, and between some people experiencing more impact than others, but also between people experiencing positive and negative changes in their well-being. This has consequences for inequality. There will also be trade-offs in the type of impact made; social or environmental; education or health; and financial or social.

Creating a formal accounting relationship would mean that these trade-offs will need to be transparent and accounted for. They exist even for an organization solely creating financial value, particularly in trading off between short- and long-term values. There is no right answer to these decisions, but more transparency and more involvement of those experiencing the changes will create a body of practice and social norms. There are various initiatives to make these trade-offs more transparent through valuation, for example the Value Balancing Alliance (VBA 2019), Harvard University's Impact Measurement Project (IWAI 2019) and Social Value International's standard on valuation (SVI 2020). These kinds of initiative are essential to help stakeholders identify what "better impact" means, and to develop common definitions and interpretations.

What to Measure?

The ability to choose between different options which may affect different groups of people in different ways means that data will be needed on all the effects, or at least the ones that matter. Deciding what matters will be a critical part of deciding what to measure, and how to measure it.

Once you decide what matters, data will be needed on the specific changes in well-being that may be experienced: data on how many people, how much change (from a baseline), over how much time. Care will be needed to ensure the reported impact relates to the activity funded. Given the potential for different changes in different outcomes for different people, the relative importance of these will need to be explicit and transparent. In summary, an account of the relative importance of material changes in well-being, positive and negative, caused by the organization.

As with financial risk, impact risk will now be a concern.

Impact accounting will need to address the risk that the information is not complete or not accurate for the stated purpose. As with finance, risk also relates to the underlying business model, the wider context, and the management team's experience. The variations in possible purpose for impact accounting make this assessment harder. Additionally, impact investing carries a larger risk, that the people whose lives are being changed are not changed as expected. The consequences of this risk are not experienced by the organization or the investor, but the people and communities they act on behalf of. Lower levels of accountability and the breakdown of the principal–agent relationship means that there will be few or no consequences if impact is not as expected. Consequently, impact risk assessment is underdeveloped and market mechanisms to manage and offset impact risk are rare. There are no secondary markets to offset impact risk, and portfolio approaches for example balancing high impact investments with a high impact risk against lower impact but lower impact risk investments are exceptional.

While there is variation in the purpose of impact accounting, there is growing convergence in the basic requirements. The Impact Management Project (IMP 2018) is facilitating a structured network of standard setters that is working toward greater convergence. Some of the organizations involved in this network include the IFC which supports principles for impact investor managing impact, Social Value International (SVI) which supports principles for the process of impact accounting, and the UNDP which is developing Practise Assurance Standards for SDG Impact (UNDP 2019). These standards will cover the practice of impact management in Private Equity, Bonds and Enterprise and include independent assurance. Also connected to the UN, the UN Global Compact and Future-Fit Foundation (FFF) are collaborating so that the SDG orientation of the former is linked more closely with the systems change thinking of the latter. FFF is also looking at how its benchmark can be used with the Sustainability Accounting Standards Board (SASB) metrics. Despite this, there are relatively low levels of reporting impact, more variability in practice, and few examples that would be consistent with emerging good practices.

However, given that there is not yet a fully established impact ecosystem (see below), and recognizing that impact accounting should reflect performance, there is a need for other metrics that allow performance to be compared. One approach is to consider the rate and extent to which organizations respond, make changes to their goods and services, in response to impact information, where those affected are the building block for that information. Accountability's Assurance standard includes Responsiveness and Keystone Accountability have developed an Improvement Rate Metric to address this.

How to Measure?

Again, the first question will be, how well to measure? Good enough for investors to make decisions in the interests of the people who get the impact. Again, consistency will be important across all the dimensions of impact covered in what to measure. Consistency will also be needed for the basis for trade-offs, comparing the relative importance of different impacts for different people. As with finance, the relationships between impacts will be dependent on their context, so consistency will not be the measure as much as the process by which it has been derived. Within organizations making their own decisions with a different perception of risk and the consequences of making the wrong decision, what will be good enough will vary.

One of the perceived challenges of measuring impact is the need for the assessment of relative importance. There is a growing body of theory and practice on how to use financial proxies to value social and environmental outcomes including the work of the Capitals Coalition, and more recently in the Value Balancing Alliance (2019) and the Impact Weighted Accounts Project at Harvard Business School.

These motivations do not necessarily require the same level of reliability for the inclusion and valuation of social and environmental outcomes. We can also assume that the investor interest in these outcomes errs on the side of inclusion rather than exclusion to give them comfort about the impact of their investments. This information can sit alongside financial accounts, and can contribute to decision-making, but it does not fully integrate with it under our current approach to accounting. That would require a more fundamental change.

Who Measures?

As with financial accounting, it will be the organization that is receiving investment and providing a good or service—in this case, causing the changes in people's lives. There is a potential conflict of interest if the organization's ability to attract and retain investment depends on the level of impact they measure and report. Especially as the people whose lives are changing are less able to hold the organization to account and the lack of consistency in how impact is defined and measured, and the lack of legislation that sets equivalent requirements for true and fair means that impact accounts are likely to over-claim impact. As with finance, the need for accounts to be audited, by someone acting on behalf of both investors and the people whose lives are changed, is fundamental but lacking.

Finance – designed for an investor who gets the financial return	Ecosystem	Impact – for an investor who doesn't get impact
Critical/Plentiful	Press	Limited
Professional bodies, CFA	Analysis	Fledgling
Legal requirements, FRC	Reporting	Rare, inconsistent
Generally accepted, IAASB	Audit	Standard but not generally accepted, in practice rare and opposed
Generally accepted, IAASB	Accounting	Convergence on principles and dimensions
Significant investor protection	Legislation	Limited, but growing

Fig. 4.6 Financial ecosystem vs. social impact ecosystem

The Wider Ecosystem

For all the reasons above, the wider ecosystem is underdeveloped compared to the financial ecosystem (Fig. 4.6). However, there are the beginnings of a comparable ecosystem. There have been some changes in legislation that have increased requirements to report on impact. There is increasing convergence around the requirements for impact accounting. There are standards that address the assurance of impact accounts for example Social Value International's Assurance standard (SVI 2019) and the IAASB is currently consulting on guidance on Assurance of Extended External Reporting (IAASB 2020) that address impact and the challenge that impact is often experienced by people who are not the intended users of impact accounts. However, there is still a long way to go to replicate the coverage of the financial ecosystem.

Nonfinancial Statements

Legislation is expecting more from directors. In the United Kingdom, directors now have to say more about how they have considered the effects of their decisions on other stakeholders. The EU nonfinancial reporting directive requires companies, albeit very large companies, to report on their impact through a nonfinancial statement.

This directive requires companies with at least 500 employees to "include in the management report a nonfinancial statement containing information to the extent necessary for an understanding of the undertaking's development, performance, position and **impact** of its activity" (European Commission 2019). Reports should cover both positive and negative impacts "in a clear and balanced way," that "reflect[s] a company's fair view of the information needed by relevant stakeholders" (European Commission 2017).

The UK Government's Civil Society strategy in 2018 stated that "central government departments will be expected to apply the terms of the Act to goods and works, and to 'account for' the social value of new procurements, rather than just 'consider' it as currently."

If investors are now deemed to be acting in the interests of people experiencing an impact, they become, in effect, the agent of those people, who are upgraded to be the principal. Enterprises report to and are accountable to their investors in an ecosystem that requires far more transparency where effects of decisions on other stakeholders have to be accounted for. This may seem a radical change but the FRC's new stewardship code (FRC 2019) has moved in this direction, raising the bar on the requirement for investors to account for environmental, social and governance (ESG) factors.

Designing an Impact System

Any impact ecosystem has to be considered in the context of the financial ecosystem. While it is possible to produce financial returns that have of themselves a positive impact, alongside any social or environmental impact, the current approach to financial accounting makes this less likely. An enterprise that has a positive impact, creates financial returns, and increases executive pay will have widened inequality and ultimately had a negative impact on SDG10. This returns us to the challenges in how impact is defined and what is considered material.

Whatever we do to address inequality, the rest of the market, currently at a substantially larger scale, will still be producing financial accounts. These accounts will continue to give price signals to investors and affect resource allocation decisions in a way that increases inequality. An impact ecosystem designed to create more impact needs to:

- Be clear about what is meant by impact, converge around one meaning, and recognize that compromises should result in more impact than holding out with a wide number of different definitions;
- Recognize choices between options and enable assessments of relative importance of different impacts;
- Have consistency, recognizing that consistency within organizations, even if not more broadly shared, is an important step;
- Address the disconnect between principal and agent, between the people paying for impact and the people getting the impact;
- Recognize that the people getting the impact are going to be interested in increasing the impact;
- Recognize that some people will resist approaches to increasing impact that have a negative effect on their perceived power and well-being;
- Share basic requirements for data in order to make comparisons and choose options that increase impact.

Bridging the Gap Between Financial and Impact Accounting

Getting impact accounting on a level with financial accounting, and established as a separate discipline, will be challenging unless legislation recognizes that the people getting the impact, whose lives are being changed, should have at least the same protection as is available to financial investors. Indeed, given that this group of people are underserved in relation to investors, perhaps they should have more protection. Not only do these people need a voice, there needs to be recognition that what they value is included in definitions of impact. If there is no agreement on what should be covered in impact, the effort put into impact accounting is unlikely match that put into financial accounting. Moreover, the organizations reporting will not be pressured to change and increase their impact with the same relentless energy that is demanded by the financial ecosystem.

New legislation and industry-led developments function to increase the quality of information provided by organizations of all types, reporting the additional information alongside the financial accounts. But despite these change, financial accounting remains immutable. The values embedded within it continue to drive resource allocation in ways that undermine impact. Those who benefit from the existing economic system reflected in financial accounting are unlikely to relinquish power and control voluntarily, and there is a risk that impact is defined and managed in ways that will not change underlying power dynamics (Giridharadas 2018). It is this unwelcome possibility that makes it important to seek out evidence that supports the notion that impact is more important than concentrating solely on financial performance.

One argument for impact accounting is that enterprises that are allocating resources in activities that take impact into account perform better. It is not the purpose here to review the literature on this, suffice to say that the jury is out and there is research that supports a relationship and research that argues there is no relationship. Challenges include the relationship between reporting and the effect on resource allocation; the relationship between specific sustainability investments where there may be data and performance, as opposed to a more holistic approach to resource allocation, where there is much less data, and performance; the risk that well-managed companies also manage sustainability issues and it is the management that drives performance; the inconsistency in what is considered as sustainability and what is included, especially effects on inequality, and so on (for example, see Kim and Lee 2018). Either the information does lead to better performance, in which case there is no reason to believe we have reached a limit for this and we can do more, or it doesn't, and given that fact, we need to address the way resources are allocated, in which case we need much more.

One of the challenges for impact and sustainability reporting more generally is that there are many stakeholders. This has led to multi-stakeholder reporting. If deciding what goes into an account for a single stakeholder is challenging, it will be so much harder when there are many stakeholders with many different purposes in mind for using the information. It may be possible to produce the information, but if the information is going to be useful and used by different people to reach different types of decision, then either the same information matters for all people and all decisions, which is unlikely, or it will be necessary to organize it so that each user can clearly identify what matters to them for a particular decision. Without this clarity there are risks that the information isn't used or that the decision is influenced by information that isn't material. And if a different decision would have been made without information that is not considered material, there is a problem.

Materiality is a debated subject in sustainability since it determines what an enterprise has to account for and potentially become accountable for. These decisions are made with reference to social norms and tested by an assurance process, acting on behalf of investors. Materiality of impact would now be outside an enterprise's control, determined by social norms tested by an audit process acting on behalf of investors now also acting in the interests of the people who experience impact.

However, there is a possible way around these challenges. Accounting can continue to have a single user in mind if that user's motivations are changed to recognize the interests of other stakeholders. Adam Smith in the *Theory of Moral Sentiments* posits that all humans recognize in themselves the interests of others:

> How selfish soever man may be supposed, there are evidently some principles in his nature, which interest him in the fortune of others, and render their happiness necessary to him, though he derives nothing from it except the pleasure of seeing it. (Smith, 1759: section 1, chapter 1, para 1)

We could decide that the basis of financial accounting is not only financial returns. There are many alternate possibilities, and to maintain the consistency that is fundamental to comparison, we will need to focus on one. This would be a fundamental change that would permit integration between financial and impact accounting.

We could argue that the basic motivation is simply to generate financial, social, and environmental returns, or perhaps financial returns subject to net positive impact or subject to no increase in inequality. This is what we try to do in thinking about future generations, arguing that our current decisions should not negatively affect future generations. For example, Islamic accounting had a different starting point, based on the interests of the community rather than on the interests of private investors and included a sense of fair and just transactions between people (Islamic accounting, 2018). (This has changed since both the Islamic Financial Services Board in Malaysia and the Accounting and Auditing Organizations for Islamic Financial Institutions (AAOIFI) have moved to align with IFRS.)

It is not necessary that these returns be easy to measure or that the inevitable trade-offs are resolvable. Even in the established uses of financial information, investors have to make trade-offs in pursuit of financial returns. The point is that the inclusion of social and environmental returns should be transparent. What might constitute norms will evolve in practice, driven by the same processes that have made it possible to standardize the judgments that are required in financial accounting—an increase in the number of accounts that address these issues, the influence of an audit process that has to consider them, and social and policy norms. If we leave financial accounting as is, preferring to add supplementary information, it will not drive behavior to the extent required. The ecosystem with its incentive salaries, bonuses and returns will continue to focus on financial value alongside a burgeoning research base for the usefulness of other data. Relying on analysts to make judgments on our behalf based on this additional, but separate, information is not only being overly trusting of their ability to make the best decisions on our behalf without clear accountability, but won't provide the level of transparency society requires.

We are used to treating financial accounting as a given and relying on laws to improve behavior. But expectations of how much laws focused on acts of commission (as opposed to acts of omission) can accomplish are probably unrealistic. Identifying potential breaches is one challenge; enforcement is another entirely. Changing the basis of accounting, rather than corporate law, would reduce the gap between enterprise behavior and society's expectations. The effect of changing the basic motivation would be that social and environmental outcomes would have to be identified, valued, and included in accounts; this is what happens with financial accounting and there is no reason for that to change.

Some people argue that valuation boils everything down to numbers, that this is part of the problem and that this level of reductionism isn't useful. Valuation is the process by which people's subjective preferences and values are made more transparent. It's not the end of the decision-making process; it means decision-making and argument start from a common place, one where valuations are at least informed by the people experiencing impact. Arguing that these values are not correct forgets that decisions are being made all the time based on far more subjective prejudices of relative value that cannot be informed by social norms. Measurement requires a common measure to compare. Even if there are a range of metrics being used, the relative importance of each in a decision is either implicit and variable or can be made transparent. Including a financial value for these outcomes also means that the choice between financial return and impact is clearer, it is on the table, and if the values are informed by the people who experience the impact it puts their values on the table in a tangible and meaningful way.

There is a possible trade-off between completeness and reliability. In finance, reliability is more important. Perhaps for impact it will be completeness that is more important in order to represent investors' motivations.

Profitability and the amount that can be distributed to owners would also be affected. Enterprises that on balance have higher negative impacts would be less attractive to the investment managers and the enterprises cost of capital would increase. This would also provide an incentive for enterprises to generate new products and services where impact considerations were automatically incorporated in design and potentially a shift in the industrial, commercial and service landscape toward business creating a far more holistic value for customers and investors.

Conclusion

The separation between impact and financial value is a social construction. It is neither inevitable nor necessary. Imagine a future where this was not the case. The Roosevelt Institute's study of neoliberalism's negative consequences for natural and social system health, and OECD's NAEC initiative examining the degenerative nature of the relentless pursuit of economic growth are examples of how impact is being reexamined. Accounting has been around for so long that it is hard to remember that it's not a given. It's not the same as a law of thermodynamics.

It's perhaps not commonly realized that accounting has chosen to exclude environmental or social value, or that it requires significant judgments about what is valuable in preparing accounts. In a recent survey, 65% of people were not aware that businesses did not have to account for social and environmental value created or lost (Thomas 2019). Financial accounting is only financial because it has been designed to deal with one perspective of investors' decision motivations, describing these as economic, with a limited definition of what economic means. There is nothing that says accounting has to be limited to economic decisions—however defined.

Through impact accounting, we can expand the underlying motivation of investment beyond a single wealth-maximizing individual to encompass the well-being of our neighbors, other communities and the planet. While financial accounting has contributed to the world's Wicked Problems by singly focusing on financial returns at the expense of people and planet, it also provides a successful model for impact investing. It provides a method for measuring value irrespective of a company's location, industry or size. It is socially constructed and global, and successful at gathering and reporting data necessary to facilitate informed choices that lead to desired outcomes and ultimately growth. Impact investing can learn from, adapt, and reimagine this system to provide accountability for those experiencing the changes driven by investment, to measure and account for how investment decisions affect people, inequality and our climate. Through its support of initiatives such as Netzwerk Plurale Ökonomik and Promoting Economic Pluralism (PEP), advances thinking about what an economy that values impact and financial value looks like, and how activities within it can be measured. Oikos's Curriculum Change Initiative also aims to prepare young people to address urgent global sustainability challenges by providing an education that fosters system thinking and heterodox, transdisciplinary economic approaches that assume strong sustainability as a prerequisite for a working economy. The Institute for New Economic Thinking at Oxford University offers a three-day intensive course—Boot Camp—to help philanthropic funders get up to speed in a non-technical way on leading-edge new economic thinking drawing on the social and physical sciences to make economics better serve humanity.

In their different ways, these initiatives are highlighting that financial accounting is not value-free and, unless changed, will continue to drive resource allocation in ways that undermine impact. Those who benefit from the existing economic system are unlikely to relinquish power and control voluntarily, and there is a risk that impact is defined and managed in ways that will not change underlying power dynamics (Giridharadas 2018). Getting impact accounting to the same state as financial accounting will require common practices and shared standards, and widespread integration in order to match the same relentless energy that is demanded by the financial ecosystem. It will also require changes in public policy, in what we think of as value and in how we hold enterprises to account in creating that value.

References

Ardor SEO. 2020. How Many Google Searches Per Day on Average in 2020? https://ardorseo.com/blog/how-many-google-searches-per-day/.

Buteau, Ellie, Ramya Gopal, and Phil Buchanan. 2014. *Hearing from Those We Seek to Help: Nonprofit Practices and Perspectives in Beneficiary Feedback*. The Center for Effective Philanthropy.

Chavez, Michael. 2020. Measuring Purpose: Merging Profitability and Social Impact at the International Finance Corporation. *Forbes*, February 24.

Clifford Chance, LLP. 2018. Initial Public Offers: A Guide to The UK Listing Regime.

Cohen, Sir Ronald. 2018. A Guide to the Impact Revolution: Our 8 Beliefs. On Impact. https://www.onimpactnow.org/our-8-beliefs/.

Concern Worldwide. 2018. Concern Worldwide Annual Report & Financial Statements 2018.

De Long, Bradford J. 1998. Estimates of World GDP, One Million B.C–Present.

Department for Digital Culture, Media & Sport. The Public Services (Social Value) Act 2012: An Introductory Guide for Commissioners and Policymakers.

European Commission. 2019. Non-financial Reporting, 2019. https://ec.europa.eu/info/business-economy-euro/company-reporting-and-auditing/company-reporting/non-financial-reporting_en.

European Commission. 2017. Guidelines on Non-financial Reporting (Methodology for Reporting Non-financial Information).

Financial Reporting Council. 2014. True and Fair.

Financial Reporting Council. 2019. The UK Stewardship Code 2020.

Foxworth, Rodney. 2018. Wealth Inequality and the Fallacies of Impact Investing. Medium: BALLE Views, February.

Gabor, Emily. 2018. Opinion: A Critical Look at the IFC's New Incentives Framework. Devex, January 4.

Gao, Yun, Xiang Gao, and Xiaohua Zhang. 2017. The 2°C Global Temperature Target and the Evolution of the Long-Term Goal of Addressing Climate Change—From the United Nations Framework Convention on Climate Change to the Paris Agreement. *Engineering, 3* (2, April): 272–278.

Giridharadas, Anand. 2018. *Winner Takes All—The Elite Charade of Changing the World*. New York: Alfred A. Knopf.

Gunelius, Susan. 2014. The Data Explosion in 2014 Minute by Minute—Infographic. ACI (blog), July 12.

Helliwell, John, Richard Layard, and Jeffrey Sachs. 2019. *World Happiness Report 2019*. New York: Sustainable Development Solutions Network.

IAASB. 2020. Proposed Non Authoritative Guidance, Extended External Reporting Assurance. IAASB.

IFRS Foundation. IFRS 15 Revenue from Contracts with Customers.

Impact Management Project. 2018. https://impactmanagementproject.com/impact-management/structured-network/.

Impact-Weighted Accounts Project at Harvard Business School. 2019. https://www.hbs.edu/impact-weighted-accounts/Pages/default.aspx.

International Finance Corporation (IFC). 2019. AIMM General Guidance Note Project Assessment and Scoring Guidance Note, March.

Kim, Kyungbok, and Sang-Myung Lee. 2018. Does Sustainability Affect Corporate Performance and Economic Development? Evidence from the Asia-Pacific Region and North America. *Sustainability* 10 (4): 909.

Oxfam. (2018). *Reward Work, Not Wealth: To End the Inequality Crisis, We Must Build An Economy for Ordinary Working People, Not the Rich and Powerful* (M. Lawson, Ed.). Oxford, UK: Oxfam International. Retrieved from https://www.oxfam.org/sites/www.oxfam.org/files/file_attachments/bp-reward-work-not-wealth-220118-summ-en.pdf.

pfc social impact advisors. 2017. The Power of Feedback: Solving Wicked Problems Through Listening and Learning.

Sarkisova, Elina. 2016. Is Feedback Smart? Feedback Labs, June 2016.

Scripps CO_2 Program. 2019. Primary Mauna Loa CO_2 Record. Scripps Institution of Oceanography, May.

Smith, A. (1759). *The Theory of Moral Semtiments* (1st Ed.). Glasgow, UK: A. Milar, and A. Kincaid and J. Bell.

Smith, Adam. 1776. An Inquiry into the Nature and Causes of the Wealth of Nations, Book IV, Chapter 2 para 4.

Smith, Murphy. 2018. Luca Pacioli: The Father of Accounting.

Social Value International. 2019. *Valuation Standard*. SVI.

Social Value International. (2020). *Social Value International Standards and Guidance - Social Value International - Open Access*. Retrieved October 16, 2020 from https://socialvalueint.org/social-value/standards-and-guidance/.

Social Value UK. http://www.socialvalueuk.org/report-database/.

Stiglitz, Joseph, Jean-Paul Fitoussi, and Martine Durand (eds.). 2018. *For Good Measure: Advancing Research on Well-Being Metrics Beyond GDP*. Paris: OECD Publishing.

The Social Progress Imperative. 2019. The Social Progress Index 2019.

Thomas, David. 2019. Should Businesses Be Forced to Include Social and Environmental Impact When Calculating Profits. Social Value UK, January. http://www.socialvalueuk.org/should-businesses-be-forced-to-include-social-and-environmental-impact-when-calculating-profits/.

Twersky, F., Buchanan, P., & Threlfall, V. (2013). Listening to Those Who Matter Most, the Beneficiaries. *Stanford Social Innovation Review* 11 (2): 41–45.

United Kingdom National Meteorological Service. 2019. Mauna Loa Carbon Dioxide Forecast for 2019.

UNDP. 2019. Practice Assurance Standards for SDG Impact. Retrieved from https://sdgimpact.undp.org/practice-standards.html.

Value Balancing Alliance. 2019. https://www.value-balancing.com/about-us/.

CHAPTER 5

The Surround Sound of Technology as an Accelerator of Social Good

Introduction

Today, we have reached a new turning point in how we use and apply technology to address Wicked Problems in a complex world. For example, as the novel coronavirus pandemic swept across the globe it hastened the need for contactless transactions which led to a greater reliance on e-commerce, digital payments, mobile money, internet banking, digital wallets, and cashless transactions. Further, travel restrictions, physical closures, and social distancing measures to reduce the spread of the pandemic increased reliance on technology for healthcare delivery, education, information, work, commerce, and connection. Driven by an urgency to solve shared global problems, in such times of global crises we also look to technology to provide life-saving tools and medicines to protect human life.

Deliberate Leadership in sociotechnical implementation is critical. It is vital that Deliberate Leaders implement safeguards needed to ensure that technological implementation does not do more harm than good. Deliberate Leaders need to have the foresight to understand the complexities of technological implementation at the individual, organizational, and global levels. As we have rushed to use technology, we have also amplified the use of existing systems and platforms, many of which are free and readily available. Yet, we have not always fully assessed underlying issues of security, privacy, and data use. Ensuring data security, data

G. Peterson et al., *Navigating Big Finance and Big Technology for Global Change*, Palgrave Studies in Impact Finance,
https://doi.org/10.1007/978-3-030-40712-4_5

privacy, management of personal information, and access are all crucial sociotechnical issues. Amid an ever-changing world, where there is still a great divide between those who have access to technology and finance, and control over its implementation, it is vital that Deliberate Leaders carefully think through the sociotechnical implications of technology.

It is also important to consider the longer-term implications of technological adoption. For instance, technology brings promise and peril when it comes to helping address global poverty and systemic change. In her 2019 article *Banking on the Future of Women*, Sarah Hendriks, Director of the Gender Equality program at the Bill & Melinda Gates Foundation, addressed the importance of digital financial services as a key part of sociotechnical solutions, in particular for 40% of women in the developing world, and who are among the world's poor. She notes, "Poverty is not a single fact or condition, but rather a collection of them: a lack of financial assets, a lack of access to property, and a lack of voice in one's community" (Hendriks 2019). She cites mobile money, debit and credit cards, and e-commerce platforms as game changing, particularly for women in the developing world. She compares for instance the situation of unbanked female garment workers in Bangladesh. In the past, they had to surrender their cash earnings to a spouse or family member and had little say over how money was being spent (Hendriks 2019). After wages became electronic, 69% of women reported more control over savings. Similarly, Liberian schoolteachers often made a 10-hour journey to obtain collect their paychecks. After wages and salaries were digitized, travel time was reduced by 90% (Hendriks 2019).

As these examples illustrate, technology as a tool holds the promise of helping people address Wicked Problems. Yet, as technical solutions grow in complexity and speed concerns regarding protections of individual rights and security, issues of self-regulation, and questions of accountability for harm grow exponentially.

In this chapter, we explore the promise and perils of specific technologies as they address Wicked Problems and the UN Sustainable Development Goals (SDGs). We discuss the difficult choices leaders face in in terms of balancing competing "needs": the transactional needs of individuals; the business need to collect personal information; and the needs to ensure the sovereignty of individuals' rights of privacy and control of data. Throughout the chapter, the principles of Deliberate Leadership offer guideposts to help leaders manage these competing interests while helping to address complex, systemic problems.

Technology as an Accelerator of Social Good

As a tool, technology can be a powerful enabler for Big Finance to do more to achieve social good. Consider three positive, poverty-alleviating technological solutions. First, expanding financial inclusion to the poor. As of 2018, an estimated 1.7 billion people comprised the world's "unbanked" (World Bank 2018). It is estimated that providing financial services to the world's poor could add more than $250 billion to global GDP. The unbanked lack financial infrastructure and access preventing them from being able to use, transfer, secure, and grow their money. Technology is seen as a way of opening up banking and financial transfer systems to the poor.

Second, technology is seen as a tool to accelerate and secure the transfer of money and aid. Today transfers of money and aid are often slow and insecure. Many aid organizations and technology companies are piloting ways to address this problem through private blockchains and common ledger technology combined with other technologies such as AI and biometrics as well as the use of cryptocurrencies.

Third, technology is being piloted to solve problems in verifying, documenting, and facilitating individual rights and executing contracts so that people have control over their property and money, and corruption is minimized.

While the tools of technology can play an important role in addressing these and other social problems, technology alone is not applicable to all sustainable development challenges. They can also bring unforeseen problems that can cause harm. This is particularly true when commercial technology solutions are adapted to complex social issues.

History shows several common technology myths including:

- **The myth of common vision.** Technology will be used in the social sphere in the same way that developers and organizations envision.
- **The myth of a common frame**. Those implementing sociotechnical solutions share a common frame of reference when it comes to ideologies, laws, policies, including common norms and ideals of freedom, individual rights, and democracy; and
- **The myth of effective self-regulation.** In the absence of laws and regulations (particularly in states with weak rule of law and among vulnerable communities) sociotechnical solutions that are implemented through means of self-regulation will be secured, monitored,

and individual rights protected such that the public is not susceptible to harm.

When these myths are treated as truth, big problems can arise. These include: the unintended use of technology, violations of privacy rights, conflicts over property and ownership rights, and issues involving control over technology. Other problems include the lack of technological security, the lack of liability for unintended harm, and problems addressing service levels and performance.

Compounding these problems is the fact that technology is inconsistently regulated under national or international law. As technology spans international borders and enters nation states with either weak rule of law, or on the flip side, overbearing restrictions, society must rely on private organizations, corporations, and consortia to self-regulate when it comes to sociotechnical decision-making. Thus, vulnerable individuals (particularly the poor and marginalized) whose individual rights are not adequately protected by local, national, and international laws and standards, and who are not developers of the technology itself, often have very little or no recourse for harm done to them as a result of sociotechnical implementation. The result, intended or not, is that the world's poor risk being exposed to a range of technologies that are not designed with their personal well-being in mind. Such technologies are designed with commercial purposes in mind, and users may be unaware of the harm they are exposed to if their personal information is collected, stored on systems of private companies or consortia, coded, and used in ways that users never intended.

Technology and the Role of Deliberate Leadership

Once the three technology myths are exposed, the need for conscious, purposeful human leadership becomes apparent. Technology cannot replace Deliberate Leadership which requires leaders to think, feel, imagine, and exercise moral judgments in finding solutions to Wicked Problems, in ways only humans can. Adoption of the Deliberate Leadership principles set out in Chapter 2 can help manage the use of technology in order to increase its benefits and reduce its harm. Highlighted throughout the chapter are the Deliberate Leadership principles necessary to harness technology for social good including **compassion** for others, seeking out **community** voices and placing them at the center of the table (i.e., the technology is in service to them not vice versa), **collaboration** with others working to address the same or related Wicked Problems, **candor** to speak the truth about what is and isn't working with a technology especially in terms of serving social good and doing no harm, and technology's support for all forms of **capital**—social, environmental and financial—to address Wicked Problems.

Before leaders undertake any technology solution, they first should answer two important questions.

- How do we ensure that revolutionary innovations and good intentions in using technology translate to meaningful progress rather than harm?
- Do we have the foresight to avoid harm to society to avoid repeating the sad refrain, "If only we'd known?"

Intentional and authentic application of Deliberate Leadership principles provides a superstructure to help answer those questions. In our research and interviews we find two things. First, that in the rush to apply technology to solve either Wicked Problems or transactional problems, leaders do not adequately address these questions up front. And, second, that liability for harm to individual rights arising from technical solutions applied to the social sphere is not adequately addressed. Answering these questions requires a new understanding of technology and the challenges of sociotechnical implementation, which is often uncomfortable to discuss, and too often not honestly addressed by technology leaders. We look at these challenges through three critical structural issues with Big Tech and Big Finance. Each raises the issue of who controls access to the technologies, and the assets and voices of those using the technologies. Essentially each challenge is about democratic control and engagement, both of which are foundational aspects of Deliberate Leadership.

Challenge 1: Control Over Technology's Implementation

The promise and perils of Big Tech is nowhere more apparent than in the issue of control. Technology's predominance in the social sphere—the proliferation of free accounts on social media, the internet, and communications and mobile technology—promises access, assets, and voice to society. But at the same time, there are perils in having technologies that are widely used and adopted by a diverse and global body of people being controlled by a handful of tech investors and tech executives who have corporate control over the implementation of technology.

This tiny group have strategic and voting control over many of the leading technology corporations, and the sociotechnical direction they take is an important issue that today's leaders from both the private and public sector must be prepared to address. For example, Tech entrepreneur founders such as Mark Zuckerberg (Facebook) (2.38B monthly users), Sergey Brin and Larry Page (Alphabet Google)—which had seven products with 1 billion users as of 2016 (Harding 2016), and other tech entrepreneurs worldwide have more powerful voting rights than other stockholders giving them voting control over their companies and their corporate and sociotechnical decisions even though the firms' economic interests are more widely held across a diversity of shareholders (Govindarajan et al. 2018).

For instance, Facebook's CEO Mark Zuckerberg controls over 50% of the voting power of Facebook. In 2016, Facebook "issued a new class of stock that [allowed Zuckerberg] … to maintain control over the company even if he sells or gives away most of his shares" (Ingram 2016). Because of Zuckerberg's voting control and final say over the company's decisions he is ultimately responsible for the company's decisions. In testimony before the United States Senate on April 10, 2018 over the privacy breach of the accounts of millions of Facebook users, Zuckerberg apologized and acknowledged his responsibility for the sociotechnical harm that arose in the privacy breach. He stated: "We didn't take a broad enough view of our responsibility, and that was a big mistake. It was my mistake, and I'm sorry. I started Facebook, I run it, and I'm responsible for what happens here" (Zuckerberg 2018).

Some tech companies such as Twitter—330 million monthly active users as of the first quarter 2019 (Statista 2020c)—do not have this share structure, but even they retain the right to issue preferred stock with special voting rights (Kafka 2013).

The practice of concentrating control over the company's decision-making by placing majority voting power in the hands of a concentrated few blends "public shares with the private-equity model—[and] many investors bristle at its undemocratic nature" (Tan and Robertson 2017).

Challenge 2: Control of Assets and Cryptocurrency

A second major issue facing not only Big Tech but also Big Finance is the role and governance of digital assets such as cryptocurrency. Explored here are the challenges, promises, and pitfalls of blockchain and distributed ledger technology that underlie digital assets.

Today there are two competing overarching visions of blockchain and distributed ledger technology that are driving its development and implementation. The "public" vision is one based on a 100% independent, distributed, decentralized, autonomous, blockchain such as the public blockchain that underlies Bitcoin. Computer scientist Roshaan Khan describes this vision as one of a supplemental world economy where "code is the law and you don't have to rely on the nature of humans" (Khan 2019). For example, Bitcoin's public blockchain is distributed, decentralized, and autonomous with its code verified by the consensus of the public at large. No single individual, group, or company can exert control over the blockchain or the verification of its code. For instance, Bitcoin and the public blockchain vision supports the notion that even if you come from a country that has hyperinflation or conflict, you could transact in bitcoin independent of the government's fiscal policy and tap into a supplemental world economy that's not reliant on national law or policy.

The second, "private" vision is just that—an organization (such as a financial institution, corporation, non-governmental organization [NGO], etc.) can have some control over who can join the network and code verification and so they use private blockchain technology or a distributed ledger technology. The vision is that private organizations can exercise some control over code verification while enjoying the benefits of a distributed ledger. Many NGOs and companies are piloting private blockchains in the social space. Consortium blockchains which combine characteristics of public and private blockchains and involve groups of organizations as well as common ledger technology such as Ripple also have greater control.

Blockchain technology and distributed ledger technology has seen a meteoritic rise in both investment and interest for its application in the social sphere. Some advocates hail it as the holy grail—a game changer for solving Wicked Problems. Yet, it comes with a set of implementation challenges as well, ones that if met with a Deliberate Leadership approach could lead to less social harm being done, and social good being optimized.

In social finance, the notion of blockchain as a force for good is largely premised on the promise that: (1) technology will be used and applied in the way that developers and investors originally intended it to be used; (2) partners, users, governments, and social impact investors share the same institutional, moral, and ethical view of how technology will and should be used, developed, and applied in the social sphere; and (3) technology is immutable and free from vulnerability. These promises form many of the core preconceptions of sociotechnical implementation. The truth is that if these promises are breached, it can bring harm to the lives and welfare of people. Furthermore, there can be a general lack of remedy for breaches that cause harm particularly in vulnerable and poor communities where not only can the rule of law be weak, but the distance (physically, technologically, culturally, ideologically, etc.) between technology developers and communities can be very great.

In Chapter 4, we mentioned that a weakness of impact accounting at present is that the intended beneficiaries of impact investing (e.g., the poor and marginalized) were excluded from the accounting process. This is in stark contrast to financial accounting, which is targeted at a particular group of stakeholders, i.e., investors. A similar weakness to do with control and accountability is apparent in cryptocurrency. When a sociotechnical initiative is launched, there is generally great enthusiasm and high hopes for success. Over time though, implementation challenges, costs, and liability for the sociotechnical program can cause service levels and performance to wane. Service levels and performance are of the major legal issues regarding the implementation of blockchain technology projects in the commercial world (McKinlay 2018). When technologies are deployed in the social space there can be even fewer financial incentives for vendors to commit to performance assurances. This is particularly true when an investor or private third party financing the project runs out of funding or loses interest in the social impact project. We find that there is very little if any insurance when social impact projects are undertaken that service levels and performance will continue in the event that a social impact investor runs out of money, resources, or loses interest in the initiative. This can cause people who choose to rely on the technology and data to be left with technology solutions that no longer are serviced or performed. This loss of access to technology and data resources can harm communities and individual's lives, health, benefits, and welfare; it is a failure of leadership.

Blockchain and Distributed Ledger Technology for Financial Inclusion

In this section we take a closer look at some examples of some of the ways that blockchain and common ledger technology is being envisioned and piloted in the social sphere. Public and private blockchains and common ledgers are being piloted and applied for financial inclusion in many sectors and in many ways. Let's look at the vision proponents have about the role of cryptocurrencies and public blockchains in achieving the vision of an alternative or supplemental economy. Of particular interest is their potential relationship to poor and vulnerable people who have escaped conflict or have been subject to the ravages of hyperinflation, lack of access to financial intermediaries, conflict, censure, corruption, modern-day enslavement, and failed economic policies which have subjected them to famine, extreme poverty, loss of identity, and despair.

In a December 2018 *Time* ideas article, Alex Gladstein, Chief Strategy Officer at the Human Rights Foundation (an NGO which itself has been an early adopter of accepting bitcoin donations) observed that facing "hyperinflation and strict financial controls, Venezuelans are adopting and experimenting with Bitcoin as a censorship-resistant medium of exchange" (Gladstein 2018). He observed that facing long food lines and rationing, no savings, censuring, and foreign wire transfer fees as high as 56%, people have few other options.

Gladstein and others see public blockchains which underlie cryptocurrencies such as Bitcoin, enabling a supplemental economy that can offer individuals an alternative to state currencies which are subject for instance to hyperinflation and ravaged domestic economies. And as a means through which they can use the peer-to-peer technology to receive bitcoin from relatives outside the country on their mobile phones. He observes that "In a refugee camp, you might not be able to access a bank, but as long as you can find an Internet connection, you can receive bitcoin, without asking permission and without having to prove your identity" (Gladstein 2018).

Gladstein acknowledges the problems of using Bitcoin and public blockchains as a new technology as it "doesn't offer cutting-edge usability, speed, or privacy." However, looking into the future he sees decentralized technologies including public blockchains as a means to provide individuals with freedom and control over their assets. It can be a "countering force" to the prospect of authoritarian regimes using "peer-to-peer digital money to create state-controlled cryptocurrencies like the Petro, which could allow them to more effectively censor transactions, surveil user accounts, and evade sanctions" (Gladstein 2018). But on the flip side, legal advocates warn that because cryptocurrencies and public blockchains operate outside of the sphere of government regulation, they can be used by corrupt organizations and individuals to advance social harm. In addition, they can be subject to volatility and are not immune from breaches of security.

Some tech leaders are advocating other alternatives to public blockchains or state-controlled cryptocurrencies to reach the world's unbanked. For example, in June 2019 The Libra Association, (a Swiss-based independent membership organization whose members include multinational companies, venture capitalists, and nonprofits which was established to manage the Libra project, currency, and transactions) published a white paper in which it outlined its plan to create "a simple global currency and financial infrastructure that empowers billions of people" (Libra 2019a). The proposal is that the Libra project, its currency, and its transactions will be managed and cryptographically entrusted to the Libra Association Initially described as "a decentralized, programmable database designed to support a low-volatility cryptocurrency", Libra was originally envisioned to be a type of global currency able to rival the major national currencies of the world (Libra 2019b). It was considered especially important for the millions of unbanked people in countries such as India—countries which also have high numbers of Facebook and related products users (Fig. 5.1).

However, the Libra has faced opposition. In 2019, Bruno Le Maire, France's finance minister held that plans for Libra's development in Europe "could not move ahead until concerns over consumer risk and governments' monetary sovereignty were addressed" (Partington 2019).

Blockchain is envisioned for other uses in the social sphere. One way is in the implementation of rights (from land and title, i.e., property, rights, etc.). Other applications include helping small businesses prove creditworthiness, and more. For example, in 2017, Coindesk reported that Arjuna Costa, a partner at Omidyar Network, observed that land registries could be a use case by which people may be able to establish property rights and title that they could use as collateral for loans (Hochstein 2017). Another use case Costa envisions is "using blockchains to analyze payment flows (including receipts and invoices) for small businesses, which would then

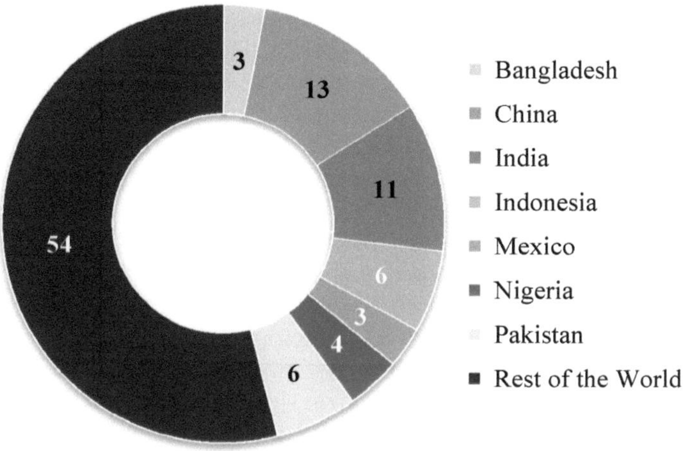

Fig. 5.1 Unbanked adults by country (%), 2017 (Adapted from Fig. 2.1, p. 36. World Bank Global Findex Database [2018])

help financial institutions to assess their creditworthiness and therefore lend to them" (Hochstein 2017).

In some cases, it is claimed that the impact of a technology is additive or transformative in and of itself. Having access to it levels the playing field of power. An example of this additive theory of technology is that the Internet, per se, democratizes access to information. Or equally technologies that help administer and speed up development aid are a de facto good. However, the situation is more complicated than it might seem. The 2017 implementation of the United Nations World Food Program (WFP) trial in using blockchain to distribute funds to refugees combined with eye-scanning hardware made by London-based IrisGuard is one example of the concerns technologists and human rights advocates have voiced in the way that blockchain technologies are being combined with other forms of data such as biometrics (iris scanning) data.

On May 1, 2017, the United Nations World Food Program launched their Building Blocks trial program in Jordan that used a private or permissioned version of the Ethereum blockchain to provide aid in the form of "cryptographically unique coupons" equivalent to a certain amount of local money to stores in five refugee camps in Jordan (Juskalian 2018). To redeem the coupons people would have their eye scanned and their personal biometric data would allow them to access the funds through the coupons (del Castillo 2017). The use of the iris scanning technology to collect personal biometric data by IrisGuard was already being used to for identity verification of more than 500,000 receiving traditional aid (del Castillo 2017). So, using the same biometric data system in this program was just seen as just a new application of that (del Castillo 2017).

Yet, social change advocates voiced their concerns particularly with respect to who controls the personal data through a private blockchain, and the hazards associated with the bulk collection of identifying information. Zara Rahman, a data and technology researcher at the nonprofit, Berlin-based, Engine Room, observed, "information and biometrics has historically been a disaster for people on the run. Think of the Holocaust, or the more recent ethnic cleansing of Rohingya in Myanmar" (Juskalian 2018).

From a sociotechnical implementation perspective, refugees as a group must submit to their biometric identifying information being captured by the private blockchain system—a system which uses their data in ways they currently have no control or say over. Russ Juskalian in the MIT Technology Review April 2018 article "Inside the Jordan refugee camp that runs on blockchain" observed that unlike a public blockchain where "anyone can join the network and validate transactions…On a permissioned blockchain, a central authority decides who can participate" (Juskalian 2018). He notes that the public blockchain consensus system "makes it difficult for any one person or agency to tamper with or forge transactions, but transaction fees tend to add up" (Juskalian 2018). The benefit of the private blockchain is that the WFP "can process transactions faster and more cheaply. The downside is that since the WFP has control over who joins its network, it also has the power to rewrite transaction histories. Instead of cutting the banks out of the equation, it has essentially become one" (Juskalian 2018).

Juskalian also raises the concern whether under such a system of biometric identification (IDs) refugees will gain ownership of their own "digital identification" or whether such systems "simply become an easier way for corporations and states to control people's digital existence" (Juskalian 2018). Further, others question whether or not other forms of identification other than biometric data such as passcodes or numbers could accomplish the identification task to protect the personal information of the individual.

Technology that decreases ownership over one's digital identity exemplifies for some the tilting of democratic control and access to information even further from communities and further serves to amplify the status quo. In this example, the decision to use biometric data was motivated by the success of the existing use of the technology for the disbursement of traditional aid. But, since individuals currently do not have complete control over their personal data and digital identification through the WFP system, does technology risk amplifying the existing inequalities of users in terms of their individual control over their own biometric data vs. institutional collection and control and private consensus? These are important types of questions for Deliberate Leaders to consider particularly in light of the complexity of sociotechnical implementation.

Property Rights and Blockchains

Examples that highlight problematic aspects of blockchain technology when it comes to social impact are a reason to consider Deliberate Leadership, not to dismiss the technologies entirely. An example where blockchain technology is increasing people's power is the administration of individual property rights. For instance, DeSoto, Inc. (an independent third-party venture) with offices in the United States and Peru led by economist Hernando de Soto and Overstock.com CEO technology entrepreneur, Patrick Byrne, are using blockchain technology "to create the world's first 'Global Property Rights Book' providing businesses, governments, and individuals better information about who has enforceable property rights over assets worldwide" (DeSoto 2019). DeSoto, Inc. stresses that its approach differs from other land rights registries using blockchain and other companies such as Factom because it has gone to local communities to collect and input existing land rights that are not formally recorded in a national registry but rather are held by local individuals under a series of local formats (Allison 2018).

At the 2018 Skoll World Forum at the University of Oxford, DeSoto, Inc. COO, Julie Smith, highlighted the sociotechnical problems that DeSoto, Inc. is trying to address. First, turning property rights into formally recorded titles can be extremely costly in many parts of the world. She observed "in Tanzania obtaining title in land takes 19 steps, 380 days, $1,443 in costs, which is a small fortune in a place where per capita GDP is $877 so who'd go through this process?" (Skoll World Forum 2018). Second, Smith noted that when people do not have their ownership rights recorded in national registries, it can place limitations on their lives. As Smith further noted, without formal ownership it is possible individuals cannot register a business, have access to the legal system, and engage in basic other human development functions (Skoll World Forum 2018).

Smith also pointed out that when property rights are not documented they can be subject to armed terrorist groups who take over a region's property (Skoll World Forum 2018). Additionally, environmental damage can occur with lack of accountability due to property not being properly recorded (Skoll World Forum 2018). Finally, particularly in post-conflict regions and/or nations which have experienced forced migration with refugees entering neighboring regions and setting up refugee camps, informal rights to land and property can be challenged. Smith points to the benefits DeSoto sees in surfacing informal ledgers including a decrease in terrorists' power over informal property rights, capital is unleashed in a widely distributed manner, and entrepreneurs with formally recorded property rights can go to work lifting the population of poverty (Skoll World Forum 2018). Technology can scale to reach millions of people at one time.

Modern Slavery and Blockchains

Humanity United (HU) is using blockchain and other technologies in a different way. A key component of the Omidyar Group, Humanity United is a private philanthropic foundation founded by Pam Omidyar (pfc social impact advisors October 2018, p. 9). Pam, and Pierre Omidyar (the founder of eBay), furnished the motivating ideas behind Humanity United—human dignity, the unity of humankind, and the need for collaborative, cooperative actions in the face of Wicked Problems.

Applying a mix of philanthropic and investment capital, Humanity United has gone all-in to make progress against forced labor. Its story is one of evolution, moving from grants with a focus on education and field building and advocacy, to one that is more focused on using and applying technology in supply chains.

Modern slavery pervades almost all countries. In 2018, the Global Slavery Index found instances of human bondage in nearly all 167 nations it studied, with North Korea, Eritrea, Burundi, the Central African Republic, and Afghanistan targeted as the worst offenders (as cited in pfc social impact advisors October 2018, p. 5). Girls and women, many of whom are caught up in human trafficking, make up 71% of victims (pfc social impact advisors October 2018, p. 5).

Supply chains, which involve a significant proportion of the estimated 16 million forced laborers (pfc social impact advisors October 2018, p. 7), have become a key focus of impact investors, including Humanity United's efforts. As supply chains for the global economy expand, with factories and other facilities located many time zones away from home offices, it is difficult to know the conditions under which workers are creating a firm's products. In some cases, management and shareholders are genuinely uninformed about the human cost involved; other times they choose simply not to find out. But in either case, it turns out to be a major problem for firms when the world finally discovers what is happening through a disaster or an investigative exposé.

Humanity United set up the Working Capital Investment Fund (Working Capital) to address the lack of technical tools to provide visibility into and enhance accountability for corporations in their own supply chains. It invests in the development of the third-party solutions—technological tools to help firms monitor and improve their own performance in combating forced labor. Publicly launched in January 2018, as of June 2020 Working Capital has eight partners—the original six, The Walmart Foundation, C&A Foundation, Stardust Equity, Open Society Foundations (Soros Economic Development Fund), The Ray and Dagmar Dolby Family Fund, and The Walt Disney Corporation—and two more limited partners, the Children's Investment Fund Foundation (CIFF) and Zalando (pfc social impact advisors October 2018, p. 18). With the UK Department for International Development contributing 2.4 million British Pounds (about US$3.5 million), Working Capital is fully capitalized at US$23 million.

As of June 2020, Working Capital has invested in nine technology companies (Provenance 2020). One of its earliest investments, Provenance uses blockchain technology that enables "brands, suppliers, and stakeholders to trace products along their journey from producer to consumer," accompanied by verified data on labor conditions that are attached to the blockchain ledger. The tool also provides workers with a secure and confidential platform for reporting on working conditions" (pfc social impact advisors October 2018, p. 22).

Prior to the investment, Provenance received an $85,000 grant from Humanity United that enabled it to pilot the tech platform focusing on

Indonesian fisheries. Since then, Provenance's blockchain technology is being used by over 200 companies (Provenance 2020).

A New Channel of Philanthropic Aid for Charities

In terms of public blockchain, cryptocurrencies such as Bitcoin are increasingly being donated by a new group of donors who have made recent wealth in cryptocurrencies and see that they can donate this property to nonprofit organizations such as The Human Rights Foundation without incurring capital gains tax and other tax implications in some jurisdictions. This has opened up a new door for NGOs and charities receiving money to fund their social missions. Yet, tracking the source of the wealth is not always possible.

Examples such as the above are encouraging for social investors interested in the role of Big Technology. However, we need to be cautious about making generalizations based on limited evidence. Perhaps one of the greatest myths of sociotechnical implementation is what is known as the fallacy of composition, "The error of assuming that what is true of a member of a group is true for the group as a whole" (Oxford University Press 2019). Applied to the sociotechnical space, for example, people may assume that if a part of the technology is secure then the whole technology system will be secure. Or, if each member of the technological implementation team is moral, then the group as a whole will produce moral outputs, etc. As demonstrated here, this is a fallacy particularly salient in the sociotechnical implementation of blockchain technology.

Challenge 3: Control of Voice and Privacy

A third challenge which has already raised its head in the previous two challenges is privacy of individual information. The right to privacy is referenced in the legal traditions of approximately 150 jurisdictions (constituteproject.org 2017). It is a right that our research found is often challenged in the implementation of commercial and sociotechnical solutions. Why is this? Privacy rights are designed to limit the actions of individuals, organizations, and governments from encroaching on individuals' private enjoyment of rights. However, the rise of technologies such as AI, the Internet, blockchain, and social media have been so rapid because of the amount of data that people are increasingly making public.

This has increased the ability of individuals, governments, and companies to collect and harvest data on individuals worldwide. As access to more data becomes more available and more integrated and accessible, the threat of compromising privacy rights grows (often in ways that system developers had not intended or anticipated). Privacy rights are often most challenged with new technologies (or in the case of social impact investing new applications of commercial technology in the social sphere) because the focus of technology leaders and sociotechnical implementers is generally not on privacy but on using technology to address other problems in the transactional environment involving scale, data capture, speed, integration, and transactions.

Historically, "privacy first" has not been the siren song of most technology implementers. Instead the focus has been on growth and the push to make more things public including connections between friends (for example, Facebook), businesses, individuals, and partners (for example, LinkedIn), and a rush to publish information online that now can be used and mined by companies, individuals, and nation states. For instance, Facebook only recently underwent a "Pivot to Privacy" after large breaches in privacy came to light (Lapowsky and Thompson 2019).

Beyond free services that people can choose to use or not use, other issues of privacy related to sociotechnical implementation concern the question: Can people truly opt out of technologies which they do not opt into but which intrude on their individual privacy? Technologies can be used for purposes of tracking and surveillance by governments, individuals, and organizations in ways that violate individual privacy rights. The European Union has legislation that strictly regulates what companies can do without the consumer's explicit consent (and the requirement is that users must "opt in" rather than "opt out"), but in much of the world—in countries rich and poor—this is not the case.

Many consumers who use search engines, e-commerce, social media, email, and other technologies do not understand the ways that companies and governments are using their data—their voice—until after a data privacy breach is revealed. Although legal disclaimers and opt out provisions may be in place, many users are driven by the need to connect to friends, colleagues, or businesses by using technology. They find it difficult, if not impossible, to maintain individual privacy rights without feeling they are being cut adrift from technologies that seem essential to live in the modern world. The challenge of protecting individual privacy rights is even greater in nation-states with weak rule of law where privacy rights are not well protected, and in developing nations where people may have very limited resources, education, and ability to opt out of technologies that are introduced.

Leaders in the social impact space must be particularly mindful of privacy rights when they apply sociotechnical solutions to address Wicked Problems. Yet, we often find that leaders are not mindful of individual privacy rights in their implementation of sociotechnical solutions. The right to privacy is too often considered by leaders to be either a right that stands in the way of growth or progress, or an individual right that can be violated in the interests of national growth or, in the context of social impact investment, a larger social objective and bringing about social change. Many projects place progress over privacy. Many individuals whose privacy rights are violated, either are not aware of the violation of their rights until after damage has occurred, or do not have the knowledge or resources to effectively seek recourse or remedy for a violation of their privacy rights.

As technologies are combined to hasten the sharing of data between and among organizations and jurisdictions, the problem of privacy protection becomes even more glaring, particularly as technology and data span both jurisdictions that do and do not recognize the individual right to privacy. Systems that combine or utilize technologies such as blockchain, social media, fintech and accounting systems, Internet/e-commerce technologies, and AI on the one hand offer the promise of doing good for communities and solving Wicked Problems, but on the other hand they can also be used for surveillance and used as instruments of oppression, violence, and abuse, to influence the outcomes of democratic elections and voting. They can even be used to curtail human rights if controlled by authorities in states with weak human rights protections or cyber adversaries.

Often technical solutions framed in the social context that are designed to solve a particular problem in the transactional environment can be used in ways other than investors and leaders intended particularly when it comes to the right of privacy. The chorus of "we didn't know what we didn't know" seems to be an all too common theme of leaders we interviewed. This increases the risk that people can do harm to others with little recourse to the person harmed. This is not the outcome that benefits society.

In the wake of events such as the 2018 revelation of the Facebook–Cambridge Analytical data breach where the personal data of millions of Facebook users was harvested without their consent, there has been talk of a "growing backlash among the public and government officials against big technology companies over privacy and transparency concerns, dubbed the tech-lash" (Murphy 2019).

Yet, while the concerns over privacy rights are both observable and widespread by leaders of sociotechnical projects, when leaders of those projects were asked about privacy rights their thinking seemed to be that the goodness of their social mission outweighed the potential harm of violations of privacy. For example, we asked, technology entrepreneurs to ask themselves the question, "it's five years or ten years down the road [from now] ... and you're testifying before Congress [about a breach of privacy rights] and you were too idealistic [about the technological solution that you put in place], what do you learn from this emerging field? What are you experiencing now that you are afraid of? .... What's getting in your way?" We found when entrepreneurs paused to answer this question, they identified either aspects of their own technology or more commonly that of another person's technology that could foreseeably cause harm to individual rights of privacy. Yet, their responses overwhelmingly seemed to suggest that the foreseeable harm to privacy was outweighed with the need to act to fill a void in the data available or to "bring change." Such thinking seems to be common.

The push to collect more data and to make it public or to structure, index, integrate, or to connect it is too often a far bigger economic, individual, and societal driver than privacy rights. And, even though leaders of sociotechnical projects we interviewed touted the societal benefits of their solutions, few addressed the issue of privacy rights. So, what do we learn from this? Well, there seems to be a general trend toward justifying the foreseeable violation of privacy rights with a broader organizational or individual mission. This is of concern to advocates of privacy rights because once privacy rights are violated there is currently very little that can be done by those harmed in terms of restitution or remedy. Although, as noted, the European Union has introduced legislation to protect individual privacy, other countries are currently not regulated in this way. Social impact leaders work at a different scale, but nonetheless they envision large-scale projects that cut across jurisdictions, and the question of how privacy rights will be protected under these projects remains open.

Another privacy issue that challenges the implementation of commercial solutions and their sociotechnical applications, involves the sharing of data between and among partners and third-party developers. This problem which occurs in the commercial sector may have similar effects on privacy rights in the social sector, insofar as third parties using data that is captured through sociotechnical initiatives in ways that were unintended.

How we safeguard the right of privacy and personal data is crucial. Individuals that favor open access argue that restricting public access in the name of individual privacy can also invite corruption. It can enable those who wish to keep private transactions that are illegal. And it can curtail public review of the data. Clearly, the issue of privacy remains a crucial issue with many far-reaching implications that leaders must consider at the outset of their implementation of technology.

Conclusion

Sociotechnical solutions confront us with new opportunities and risks. We have seen in this chapter that there are several features of technology (both positive and negative) that are replicated when a commercial technology is repositioned in a social setting. These can include the ability to speed up transactions, the ability to store and combine data in ways that can provide users with new insights, and new ways to communicate. Yet, we have also seen how vital it is that those implementing the technology take a broader view of technology such that they protect the privacy, security, property, and human rights of users. They need to ensure that vulnerable communities, who may not have a role in the development of the technology, are given a voice that is heard at the top. Technology leaders must also take responsibility for their platforms and solutions so that they are used for good and not for bad. Social change and technology experts need to know more about each other's fields. In particular, they need to know that there can be different forms of capital and different forms of shareholder control of technology companies that can accelerate certain approaches to sociotechnical solutions across these fields that may bring about diverse sets of outcomes both positive and negative when the technology is implemented and grows to include a large global user base. We have examined how crucial the leadership practice of taking a broader view of technology is in influencing social change. And, we have discussed the myths and realities of sociotechnical implementation.

Technology's implementation in the social sphere requires leadership that seeks out many voices before they act, who engage the communities to be affected by their technologies, who are candid about what is and is not working with their technology. This applies equally to situations where technology is used for a specific social purpose, and ones where the technology is held to be the improvement and its unintended or unanticipated side-effects are ignored (adaptive technology). Leaders involved in technical implementation must have the foresight to understand the role of their technology in the broader social sphere and the good and the bad that can result from the sociotechnical strategies and choices that they make.

References

Allison, Ian. 2018. Hernando de Soto and Patrick Byrne's Mission to Put the Developing World's Property Rights on a Blockchain. *International Business Times UK*, August 28. https://www.ibtimes.co.uk/hernando-de-soto-patrick-byrnes-mission-put-developing-worlds-property-rights-blockchain-1651605.

constituteproject.org. 2017. *Read About 'Right to Privacy' on Constitute.* https://www.constituteproject.org/search?lang=en&key=privacy.

del Castillo, Michael. 2017. A Branch of the UN Just Launched Its First Large-Scale Ethereum Test. CoinDesk (Blog), May. https://www.coindesk.com/the-united-nations-just-launched-its-first-large-scale-ethereum-test.

DeSoto, Inc. 2019. DeSoto Inc. https://www.desoto.com/.

Gladstein, Alex. 2018. Why Bitcoin Matters for Freedom. *Time*, December 28. https://time.com/5486673/bitcoin-venezuela-authoritarian/.

Govindarajan, Vijay, et al. 2018. Should Dual-Class Shares Be Banned? *Harvard Business Review*, December 3. https://hbr.org/2018/12/should-dual-class-shares-be-banned.

Harding, Xavier. 2016. Google Has 7 Products With 1 Billion Users. *Popular Science*, February 1. https://www.popsci.com/google-has-7-products-with-1-billion-users.

Hendriks, Sarah. 2019. How Digital Financial Services Are Empowering Women. *IMF Finance & Development Magazine*. https://www.imf.org/external/pubs/ft/fandd/2019/03/how-digital-financial-services-are-empowering-women-hendriks.htm.

Hochstein, Marc. 2017. Blockchain for Inclusion? Gates Foundation Strikes Tepid Tone at Money2020. CoinDesk (Blog), October 23. https://www.coindesk.com/blockchain-inclusion-gates-foundation-strikes-tepid-tone-money2020.

Ingram, Mathew. 2016. Mark Zuckerberg's Absolute Control Over Facebook Is Not New. *Fortune*, December 13. http://fortune.com/2016/12/13/zuckerberg-facebook-lawsuit/.

Juskalian, Russ. 2018. Inside the Jordan Refugee Camp That Runs on Blockchain. *MIT Technology Review*, April 12. https://www.technologyreview.com/s/610806/inside-the-jordan-refugee-camp-that-runs-on-blockchain/.

Kafka, Peter. 2013. One Thing Twitter Won't Have When It Goes Public: Two Classes of Shares. Dow Jones & Company Inc., October 3. http://allthingsd.com/20131003/one-thing-twitter-wont-have-when-it-goes-public-two-classes-of-shares/.

Khan, Roshaan. 2019. Author Interview with Roshaan Khan, Blockshop. Washington, DC, June 20.

Lapowsky, Issie, and Nicholas Thompson. 2019. Facebook's Pivot to Privacy Is Missing Something Crucial. *Wired*, March 6. https://www.wired.com/story/facebook-zuckerberg-privacy-pivot/.

Libra.org. 2019a. Libra White Paper | Blockchain, Association, Reserve. https://libra.org/en-US/white-paper/.

Libra.org. 2019b. The Libra Blockchain. https://developers.libra.org/.

McKinlay, John, et al. 2018. Blockchain: Background, Challenges, and Legal Issues. DLA Piper, February 2.

Murphy, Hannah. 2019. Mark Zuckerberg Calls for More Regulation of Big Tech. *Financial Times*, March 30. https://www.ft.com/content/0af70c80-5333-11e9-91f9-b6515a54c5b1.

Oxford University Press. 2019. Fallacy of Composition | Definition of Fallacy of Composition in English by Oxford Dictionaries. Oxford Dictionaries | English. https://en.oxforddictionaries.com/definition/fallacy_of_composition.

Partington, Richard. 2019. France to Block Facebook's Libra Cryptocurrency in Europe. *The Guardian*. September 12. https://www.theguardian.com/technology/2019/sep/12/france-block-development-facebook-libra-cryptocurrency.

pfc Social Impact Advisors. 2018. *Launching the Working Capital Fund. A Case Study of Humanity United* (G. Peterson, Ed.). St. Paul, MN: Oxford Impact Investing and Social Finance Programmes.

Provenance. 2020. https://www.provenance.org//.

Skoll World Forum. 2018. *The Blockchain, Artificial Intelligence and the Future of Impact Finance*. Skoll World Forum 2018. https://www.youtube.com/watch?feature=youtu.be&v=82nOf3CZpYk&app=desktop.

Statista. 2020c. Number of Monthly Active Twitter Users Worldwide from 1st Quarter 2010 to 1st Quarter 2019. https://www.statista.com/statistics/282087/number-of-monthly-active-twitter-users/.

Tan, Andrea, and Benjamin Robertson. 2017. Why Investors Are Fretting Over Dual-Class Shares. *Bloomberg Business Week*, July 10. https://www.bloomberg.com/news/articles/2017-07-10/why-investors-are-fretting-over-dual-class-shares-quicktake-q-a.

World Bank. 2018. Global Findex Database 2017. https://globalfindex.worldbank.org/.

Zuckerberg, Mark. 2018. *Hearing Before the United States Senate Committee on the Judiciary and the United States Senate Committee on Commerce, Science, and Transportation April 10, 2018.* Testimony of Mark Zuckerberg Chairman and Chief Executive Officer, Facebook. US Senate, April 10. https://www.judiciary.senate.gov/imo/media/doc/04-10-18%20Zuckerberg%20Testimony.pdf.

CHAPTER 6

From Theory to Practice

UBS and UBS Optimus Foundation

UBS Group AG (UBS) is one of the world's largest financial institutions, with US$3.2 trillion AUM encompassing the world's largest wealth manager, the largest bank in Switzerland, a specialized and successful investment bank, and a major asset management house (pfc social impact advisors 2018, p. 9). A public company incorporated under the laws of Switzerland, UBS is committed to creating a positive impact for its clients, employees, investors, and society (pfc social impact advisors 2018, p. 9). As of December 2017, UBS' sustainable investments accounted for more than a third of its total invested assets, amounting to 1.1 trillion Swiss Francs (CHF), about US$1.13 trillion (UBS AG, 2018). The Dow Jones Sustainability Indices confirmed UBS as the industry leader for the fourth year running in 2018 (pfc social impact advisors 2018, p. 9).

UBS established UBS Optimus Foundation (UBSOF, Optimus, or Foundation) in 1999 as an independent charitable grantmaking organization. Its mission is to "ensure children are safe, healthy, educated, and ready for their future" (as cited in pfc social impact advisors 2018, p. 13). Headquartered in Switzerland, Optimus has staff in Hong Kong, the United Kingdom, Germany, and the United States and includes two additional legal entities, UBS Optimus Foundation Deutschland and UBS Optimus Foundation United Kingdom; a donation platform through a

G. Peterson et al., *Navigating Big Finance and Big Technology for Global Change*, Palgrave Studies in Impact Finance,
https://doi.org/10.1007/978-3-030-40712-4_6

donor-advised fund in the United States; and a branch of the Swiss foundation in Hong Kong (pfc social impact advisors 2018, p. 14). Together, they form the UBS Optimus Network ("the Network"). The Network receives funds from UBS clients, UBS employees, and UBS. The Foundation guarantees that 100% of all donations go to projects in the areas of education, health, and child protection, because UBS covers all operating costs.

In 2017, Optimus reached more than 2.1 million children by supporting more than 175 programs worldwide (pfc social impact advisors 2018, p. 13). It also raised and disbursed US$62 million for programs focused on health, child protection, education, early childhood development, and emergency response (pfc social impact advisors 2018, p. 13). Social finance represents a small part of the Foundation's total budget; an estimated 14% or US$8.7 million was allocated for social finance in 2017 (pfc social impact advisors 2018, p. 13).

The Foundation is authorized to allow the social finance portfolio to be up to 50% of the grantmaking budget. Expansion depends on the success of programs (returns) and the continued UBS client interest in supporting social finance initiatives. The Foundation builds its own capacity and skill set by blending staff expertise in business, international development, and social change within the Foundation and the bank. It is also putting these skills to use in products that are results-based and business-oriented such a pay-for-success models.

According to UBS CEO Sergio P. Ermotti, "the Foundation was brought up and created under the umbrella of wealth management, so the idea was: 'Let's do some things that are right for society,'... and that (idea) was driven by something we felt wealthy clients wanted to do in different parts of the world—to help them to fulfill their desire to contribute to society in a structured way, not just by doing charity, but by doing it in a way that would deliver social and financial returns" (pfc social impact advisors 2018, p. 14). In 2018, UBSOF refined its strategy to focus on a three-phased approach—drive outcomes at scale, scale social business, and build the field of social finance. Specific efforts in the first of these three phases are detailed next.

Drive to Scale with Development Impact Bonds

UBSOF has focused its pay-for-performance pilots primarily on Development Impact Bonds (DIBs). These results-based contracts provide upfront by working capital by investors who are paid back by outcome funders such as government and other funders, but only if results are achieved (pfc social impact advisors 2018, p. 16). The financial risk is borne mainly by the investor. The investor will not be repaid by the outcome payer unless the implementing partners achieve negotiated, verified outcomes. The implementing partners do not have to worry about repaying a loan; thus, they have less financial incentive to only select beneficiaries that will help meet the performance outcomes. That said, outcome payers may provide incentives or bonus payments to the implementing partners if the performance outcomes are exceeded.

DIBs uniquely hybridize philanthropy and investing, and some donors see this model as a mix that works well to blend social change goals with their investment objectives. Key partners in a DIB include the service provider or implementing partner (the agency responsible for delivering the result), and the third-party verifier of results, and the beneficiary. UBSOF's DIB model captures each of these partners (see Fig. 6.1).

Because investors provide funding—and assume risk—for interventions that can lead to improved social outcomes, DIBs have the potential to attract funding for interventions that donor agencies and governments might not be willing, or able, to provide directly.

In the case of UBSOF, it is clear about its risk exposure. Tom Hall, Head of UBS Client Philanthropy Services, notes:

> From a financial risk perspective, if you're viewing the investment as a recyclable grant, the risk you're comparing it with is the minus 100% return on a grant, which often has no evidence of an outcome. In an impact bond, a donor can probably educate a child and get their capital back with a small return to re-invest in a new program, which is pretty cool. (pfc social impact advisors 2018, p. 18)

One of the key lessons learned from the two completed DIB prototypes—one in Peru and the second in India (discussed below)—is the recognition that going to scale requires government partnership and a continuation and expansion of the pilot. In addition, it was recognized that in order for NGOs to fully engage in outcome-based models, their capacity must be built, and a new culture that blends private sector skills must be woven into the social change organization's culture.

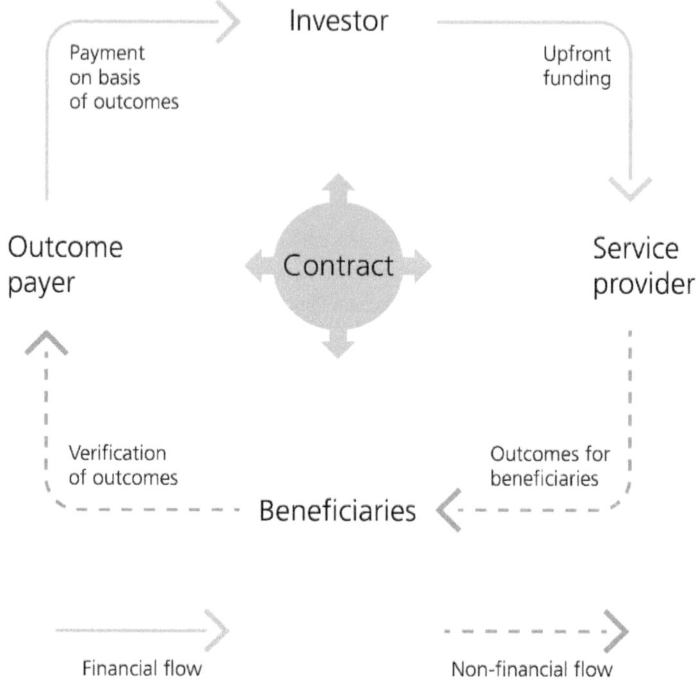

Fig. 6.1 UBSOF DIB Model (*Source* [pfc 2019] UBSOF, 2017)

UBSOF's DIBs

Three of UBSOF's Development Impact Bonds—the problems they were addressing, their locale, their impacts and the role of technology—describe how one of the largest global financial firms engaged with issues contributing to poverty.

Educate Girls Development Impact Bonds

India has the lowest literacy in the world, with compulsory education for children ages six to 14 only mandated in 2009 (pfc social impact advisors 2018, p. 22). Moreover, the resources available for education in urban versus rural areas are starkly different. These factors, combined with entrenched gender roles, have made rural girls' education virtually inaccessible. In Rajasthan, the quality of education for women and girls is poor. The state accounts for over nine percent of the 3.8 million out-of-school girls countrywide and is home to nine districts (out of 26) with the worst gender gap indicators (Bukhari and Husain 2016). As of 2016, more than 60% of out-of-school children were girls; only 55% of schools had girls' restrooms, and for every 100 rural girls who entered primary school, only 12 went on to class 12—equivalent to senior year in high school in the United States (pfc social impact advisors 2018, p. 22).

Other barriers to making improvements include bureaucratically run schools; low-quality educators and curricula; a shortage of teachers; a lack of parental involvement; and rigid societal norms that prevent girls from excelling in, or in some cases even attending, school (pfc social impact advisors 2018, p. 22). A Brookings Institute report, "Primary Education in India: Progress and Challenges" found teacher attendance in primary schools to be 85%, and the nation faces a shortage of 689,000 teachers. School principals often lack certifications or the educational training necessary to best handle management responsibilities, and a lack of remedial support means poorly performing students don't have the opportunity to catch up with their peers (pfc social impact advisors 2018, p. 22). When schools are run badly, some parents feel justified in pulling their children out of them. When parents can afford private school, they will often only send one child and will choose a son over a daughter (pfc social impact advisors 2018, p. 22).

Educate Girls

Educate Girls (EG) is a nonprofit organization based in Mumbai devoted to girls' education as a means of improving the formal economy through gainful employment that will lift their families out of poverty. It mobilizes communities and leverages government's investment in girls' education in India by providing quality education to girls in the rural Indian states of Rajasthan and Madhya Pradesh. With an education, girls are more likely to "enter the formal economy, gain employment, and lift their families out of poverty" (pfc social impact advisors 2018, p. 22). Educate Girls seeks to promote the idea of girls' education not only to the child, but also to her family and community as it attempts to shift the established cultural mindset. This approach has resulted in 200,000 out-of-school girls enrolling in education programs, transforming families and communities (pfc social impact advisors 2018, p. 22).

Educate Girls had first learned of Development Impact Bonds in 2011, when the UK Department for International Development (DfID) requested proposals for a Pay-By-Results (PBR) initiative. Though DfID pulled India from its area of consideration, Educate Girls Executive Director and Founder Safeena Husain noted that the organization "had become so invested in the PBR mechanism" that they decided to pitch it to other investors including UBSOF (pfc social impact advisors 2018, p. 22).

USBOF CEO Phyllis Costanza remembers an early conversation with Husain. "I met Safeena Husain, who runs Educate Girls, and she told me about this new thing called the Development Impact Bond. She explained it to me, and I was so excited. I thought, 'Wow! This addresses some critical issues that we're seeing in the sector'" (pfc social impact advisors 2018, p. 22).

With the idea in place, the DIB's ultimate goal—to improve education, directly and indirectly, through improvements in targeted schools for 15,000 children, 9000 of them girls, in 166 schools in 140 villages in Rajasthan's Bhawar District—emerged.

The DIB: Partners, Committed Financing, and Measurable Results

To make it happen, however, required a team and an ecosystem of skilled partners. UBSOF knew its role wouldn't be to hire teachers or to choose the curriculum. Those tasks would be up to Educate Girls. Nevertheless, UBSOF brought in resources that EG didn't have, such as scaling expertise, investor base expansion advice, and much-needed funding. Other partners played critical roles, including outcome payer, performance manager, and outcome evaluator.

The Partners

Who were these partners, and what did they bring to the table? Understanding the background of the five key participants in addition to UBSOF—the investor—explains what they each brought to the DIB, and may explain the motivations for each participant:

- **The Service Provider**: Educate Girls.
- **The Outcome Player**: The Children's Investment Fund Foundation (CIFF) is an independent philanthropic organization, headquartered

in London with offices in Nairobi and New Delhi. CIFF paid back UBSOF, as long as targets were met.

- **The Project Manager**: Instiglio provided technical advice, as well as performance management assistance to Educate Girls on behalf of UBSOF. A nonprofit intermediary based in Bogota, Colombia, it provides technical assistance in the design, structuring, and performance management of results-based financing programs in developing countries.
- **The Outcome Evaluator**: IDinsight validated the number of out-of-school girls involved and measured the outcomes. An impact evaluation firm headquartered in San Francisco with offices in India, Uganda, and Zambia, IDinsight's mission is to help policymakers and practitioners use rigorous data and evidence to make more socially impactful decisions (pfc social impact advisors 2018, p. 25).
- **The Process Evaluator**: Dalberg is a global development consultancy. As the fifth partner, its role was to reach and evaluate the processes used to plan, implement, and evaluate the DIB.

Financing and Payments

Financing the Educate Girls DIB involved payments between the investor (UBSOF), the service provider (Educate Girls), and the outcome payer (CIFF), as well as fees to support evaluation, communication, and other associated functions. UBSOF (investor) provided the working capital for the Educate Girls DIB through a three-year grant of US$270,000. CIFF (the outcome payer) committed to a payment based on performance, up to a maximum of US$422,000. UBSOF's internal rate of return (IRR) varied based on performance, running from a minus 29% to a plus 15%. EG would receive part of that payment based on performance.

Accounting for both the direct payments and support costs, the three-year DIB's total expenditures were almost US$1.1 million. Structured as a pilot, there was a clear understanding that the transaction costs would outweigh the programmatic ones. The goal was to test the feasibility of the instrument and learn from it to build the subsequent ones more effectively and efficiently.

Two performance, pay-for-results, metrics were tracked by the outside evaluator—educational achievement (i.e., learning) and enrollment. The heavily weighted former metric was based on meeting ASER standards for math competency and English and Hindi literacy; the latter was based on enrollment of 768 girls by the third year—surpassing the original goal of 79% of the 837 eligible girls (UBS Optimus Foundation 2017; pfc Social Impact Advisors 2018). In addition to measuring results in the schools in which Educate Girls was operating, the outside evaluator and Educate Girls compared those results to a set of non-serviced schools. To reduce bias, both populations of schools (those served by Educate Girls and those that were not) were randomly selected.

Results, Outcomes, Success

The Educate Girls DIB is considered a success. The Foundation earned a 15% internal rate of return, students significantly increased their reading and math levels, and 92% of eligible out-of-school girls in the target region were enrolled in school. The success rates for those two social goals were 160% of the learning performance target and 116% of the enrollment target. Educate Girls more than exceeded its target metrics. Moreover, compared to a control group, students in EG's program schools had 28% larger learning gains, with relatively higher gains in math and English. Learning gains in Hindi weren't as significant (Brookings Institution 2018).

Ultimately, the Educate Girls DIB helped to provide a quality education for 15,000 students—3000 fewer students than was projected at the start of the DIB. UBSOF recouped its initial funding of US$270,000 plus a 15% internal rate of return from Children's Investment Fund Foundation (CIFF), the outcome payer. EG received 32% of the internal rate of return, and the rest was recycled into other UBSOF programs (pfc social impact advisors 2018, p. 31).

Success for the DIB did not occur on a smooth trajectory over the three years. Year One was spent getting into a rhythm and testing out educational strategies. Year Two saw a series of course corrections that led to enrollment of 87.7% of the targeted out-of-school girls enrolled in school, with 54% of them over 10 years old (pfc social impact advisors 2018, p. 31). Yet at the end of Year Two, only 52% of students had met learning gain targets, thus more changes were made in Year Three. As EG's Senior District Manager Vikram Solanki noted, "We started conducting rigorous and more frequent assessments and gap analyses for each child in Year Three to track outcomes. This helped us figure out micro-errors, and child-specific interventions were rolled out accordingly" (pfc Social Impact Advisors 2018). The changes worked, by the end of Year Three, EG well surpassed its goals. The massive improvements in Year Three—about a 79% increase in grade levels—essentially means students absorbed the equivalent of two years' worth of instruction in one school year (pfc social impact advisors 2018, p. 31).

The Educate Girls DIB pilot provided a wealth of lessons learned that were later incorporated into its other DIBs, and they will be used to inform the implementation of the new Quality Education DIB in India.

The Brookings Institution finds the adjustments made between Years Two and Three as particularly significant: "With the learning outcomes lagging in Year Two, several adjustments were made to the intervention to boost students' success." These adjustments included structural changes in delivery (such as increased number of sessions), aligning teaching groups with competency levels, and improved curriculum content that emphasized personalized learning (pfc social impact advisors 2018, p. 32).

Lesson 1: Listen to, and Engage with, Community

Success in enrolling girls required Educate Girls and its partners to deeply engage with the communities and girls' families—both to identify girls and to earn the trust of their families. As Husain notes,

> Essentially, it's about mindset change, because everything to do with gender is underpinned with mindset. So, we go door-to-door and we find every single girl who is not in school, either dropped out or never enrolled, and this is done with our community volunteers. And once we identify them, we actually work—either through village meetings, neighborhood meetings, and/or individual parent counseling—to bring them back into school, and then to make sure that they are staying and learning (as cited in pfc social impact advisors 2018, p. 27)

On-the-ground community volunteers, known as "Team Balika" (a word that translates to "young girl"), carried out a door-to-door canvas of 34,000 households. Volunteers met with parents to try to convince them that giving their daughters an education would help their families and their communities more than their child's work at home. Often, volunteers held village meetings to inform leaders and parents about EG's work and to address any concerns they had; the meetings were meant to facilitate community conversation about girls' education.

This early, intimate, and authentic community engagement—a key characteristic of a Deliberate Leader—was pivotal to the successful outcomes of the Educate Girls DIB. Alison Bukhari notes, "We were so close to the community and really, really listening in that final year…so it was in that proximity where the success really lay" (as cited in pfc social impact advisors 2019, p. 27). Bukhari notes that listening to the community can be simple or complex. It can involve focused village or group meetings and months of data, or it can be as simple as observing the students or asking the teachers in one classroom what topics they need some extra help with understanding.

Lesson 2: Build Early Alliances with Other Local Partners—Government and Teachers

Reaching out early to government agencies, potential service providers, outcome payers, and other stakeholders was also critical to the Educate Girls DIB's success. For example, while Educate Girls did communicate with the local government and got an MOU signed with the Government of Rajasthan, it would have been helpful to have had greater up front advocacy and investment by Educate Girls and other stakeholders to help ensure adequate government support throughout the DIB. This may have lowered transaction costs and improved outcomes.

Learning to be more intentional in its collaboration—another Deliberate Leadership behavior—proved extremely useful in allowing UBSOF to begin structuring a timeline several years before the launch of its new Quality Education DIB in other parts of India.

Supporting and training teachers were another set of critical elements for Educate Girls. Its learning curriculum for all children (girls *and* boys) in third, fourth, and fifth grades was intended to make sure that they were actually learning and moving forward. To ensure the curriculum was understood and followed, Educate Girls worked closely with teachers. It wanted to support them and ensure they had the skills and mindset necessary to achieve the learning performance goals. For example, teachers came to Educate Girls saying their students weren't improving much in English literacy. The reason, the teachers explained, was because the teachers themselves didn't have enough English language teaching experience. Educate Girls provided the teachers with career training in English literacy, and their pupils' scores began to rise (pfc social impact advisors 2018, p. 27).

The Next Step: Using Technology to Scale

The success of Educate Girls DIB was notable because it surpassed targets for enrollment and learning outcomes. According to Alison Bukhari, Educate Girls' UK Director, EG is "reflecting and institutionalizing the best practices that emerged out of the DIB across 25,000 schools" (as cited in pfc social impact advisors 2018, p. 38). She notes that, "Our expansion over five years sees us double our current scale (from 15 to 31 educationally 'backward' districts as defined by the Government of India) and triple our outreach (from five million to over 16 million children)."

To achieve this scale, EG has had to answer some very basic, yet daunting questions. Ben Brockman of IDinsight (the Outcome Evaluator) offers three key questions; the answers to which all involve appropriate use of technology.

1. **With 650,000 villages and 4.1 million out-of-school girls in India, how do you predict which villages need EG most?** Brockman asserts that machine learning can predict which villages have the most out-of-school kids. Data from the government indicated that most out-of-school girls were from a small fraction of villages, but it was hard to predict where. They knew that half of the 650,000 villages contained 96% of out-of-school girls, and that 40% of all out-of-school girls are in five percent of villages. Using machine learning to predict which villages have the most out-of-school kids, IDinsight predicts that Educate Girls' field teams can reach 60% more out-of-school girls for the same cost it is spending now. It is messy business, however as the necessary data sets are difficult to merge and standardize, and the data can be noisy.
2. **Which version of the program do you scale?** At scale, small decisions add up to Big impact such as determining the frequency of in-home visits, selecting which age groups of out-of-girls on which volunteers should focus, or balancing the intensity of volunteer training versus the cost. Brockman suggests that EG can quickly determine the optimal answer for each of these by using rigorous, rapid computer-based comparison tests between various scenarios for each.
3. **How do you manage a program at massive scale?** Educate Girls will need to manage thousands of paid staff and tens of thousands of volunteers. Managing quality of service and response times from

> managers to the field requires an integrated data system, one that provides actionable data at all levels of decision-making. Establishing the right metrics and the right dashboards of those for the right level of decision-makers requires the right systems, software, and tools. Executives need dashboards that provide high-level snapshots of program performance; mid-level managers need dashboards that can identify high performers and problem areas, and field staff using smartphones need real-time data on where to focus efforts.

The answers to scale require the compilation and analysis of massive amounts of government data on schools; and the collection, management, and analysis of data from the EG field workers. The kind of social change at scale EG envisions requires technology to complement the partnerships with communities, governments, teachers, and others.

Future-Fit Foundation

Big Finance and Big Tech have created bright new opportunities to support positive social change as we have seen in previous chapters. But we have also seen there is a dark side to the impact of technology and finance and the role they are playing regarding rising inequality, fractured social and political institutions, and accelerating climate change. As we have emphasized throughout this book, the kinds of challenges Big Finance and Big Tech have to confront if they are to have meaningful social and environmental impact are messy, systemic, and large. They are Wicked Problems that do not lend themselves to simple solutions: the solutions, insofar as they are understood, are complicated and maybe irreconcilable with each other. The Future-Fit Foundation offers a way to understand and take action to address Wicked Problems. It is relevant to all industries, but it advocates a particular role for Big Finance in advocating for and enabling purposeful change.

The Foundation provides a response to issues raised in earlier chapters. For instance, it gives a basis for detecting greenwashing of the kind mentioned in Chapter 1; it helps address the comparability of companies issue raised in Chapter 3; and it offers a way of dealing with impact measurement as highlighted in Chapter 4. As we will also see, there are Deliberate Leadership dimensions to the Foundation's way of working, and companies that follow its guidance may be less likely to be unaware of the kinds of business risk discussed in Chapter 5.

Future-Fit Foundation's Approach

Company reporting on environmental, social, and governance challenges has increased rapidly over the last fifteen years, but when companies talk about their ESG performance, they are telling a story of what they have done in the past; they are not necessarily saying anything about the journey they are on and the direction they are taking. In fact, the more reporting that takes place, the harder it can be to make sense of what companies are achieving. In Chapter 2, we highlighted that there was a lack of standard rules for assessing nonfinancial performance, especially when it came to social and governance metrics. In Chapter 4, we also pointed out that measuring impact was a particular problem. Barker and Eccles (2018) cite studies that found 248 mandatory sustainability reporting instruments in use in 19 countries and regions (up from 35 in 2006), and 135 voluntary reporting instruments being used in 71 countries/regions (up from 25 in 2006). Ten years ago, the problem was the lack of nonfinancial reporting; now it is the quality of that reporting and the lack of standardization that causes reports not to be comparable, verifiable, or understandable.

Future-Fit Foundation (FFF) was established in 2013 to help companies and their investors make sense of the direction they were taking when it came to sustainability, and how far they were along that journey. It was founded at a time when companies were starting to complain about ESG report overload, the result of information being asked by multiple organizations using diverse formats that did not lend themselves to comparability. It was not just the repetition that was frustrating: it was also that the reporting only resulted in incremental change at a rate that was out of step with what was needed to tackle Wicked Problems in a timely fashion. It was as if corporate leaders were on a journey without the equipment to understand where they were heading and what route to take to get there. Moreover, a lot of the time companies talked about (i.e., reported upon) how well they were doing now compared with the past (e.g., CO_2 emissions; waste; water consumption). Reporting did not help them recognize where they needed to be if they were to contribute meaningfully to sustainable systems.

FFF's approach to helping companies manage sustainability is based on systems thinking, and the notion that there are social and natural boundaries that cannot be crossed if a prosperous, regenerative world is to be built. A Future-Fit Society is one which protects the possibility that humans and other life will flourish on Earth forever, by being environmentally restorative, socially just, and economically inclusive (pfc social impact advisors 2019). Systems thinking helps us understand how different phenomena interact in pursuit of a common purpose. It allows us to move away from individual issues toward interconnectedness, and is therefore particularly relevant for Wicked Problems. When systems thinking is applied to sustainability, what emerges is a series of nested dependencies. There are natural systems—ones that exist in nature, independent of any human involvement—and there are social systems that depend on healthy natural systems in order to flourish.

Natural systems can only flourish if certain thresholds are not crossed. For example, too much carbon dioxide in the atmosphere will lead to irreversible climate change; too many chemical pollutants can cause genetic damage to life-forms. These thresholds are also known as planetary boundaries. People need these natural systems for three purposes:

- The life-support function (e.g., air, water, a climate conducive to crops)
- The resource function to provide materials and energy, both renewable and finite
- The waste function to assimilate waste (e.g., plastic, carbon dioxide, nitrogen compounds).

Social systems are nested within natural systems. A social system that damages the life-support function, uses natural resources at unsustainable rates, and produces too much waste for the Earth to assimilate is not one that will ultimately allow humans to prosper. In addition, it risks undermining people's ability to meet their basic needs (e.g., food, shelter) and also pursue higher needs (e.g., a sense of meaning, creativity). Not only will it overshoot planetary boundaries, but it will undershoot on establishing the social foundation's humans need to flourish.

The Future-Fit Foundation Business Benchmark

A world where natural and social systems both flourish is one that is fit for the future, hence the name of the Future-Fit Foundation. Using systems science to define the essential components of sustainability, it

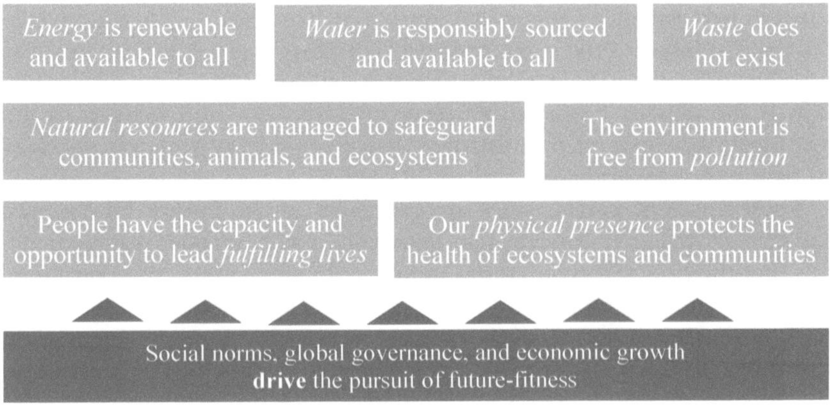

Fig. 6.2 Principles of a Sustainable World (*Source* Adapted from pfc social impact advisors [2019], Future-Fit Foundation 2019)

has identified eight core properties that need to be present in a flourishing world (Fig. 6.2). For example, in a Future-Fit Society all energy comes from renewable sources, and everyone has access to it. Likewise, the social foundations will exist to enable people to live fulfilling lives. Business is one of many institutions that make up social systems. The Future-Fit Foundation specifically targets business as a change agent in the transformation to a new kind of system. In that system, the importance of business is not the value it brings to shareholders, or how it offsets harm it causes by adding value elsewhere (cf. 'shared value'): the importance of business is to add value to natural and social systems—its significance stems from how it sustains and improves those systems. As FFF co-founder, Martin Rich, puts it, "***Business should be the servant of society, not the other way around. That for me is the essence of value***" (pfc social impact advisors 2019).

FFF wants to give to companies is a way of helping them create system value so that they contributed to building a Future-Fit Society, i.e., one which protects the possibility that humans and other life will flourish on Earth forever, by being environmentally restorative, socially just, and economically inclusive. Geoff Kendall, the second of FFF's co-founders, says "My ambition when we started Future-Fit was that within ten years every major company in the world would report on their extra-financial performance as concisely, credibly, and comparably as they do with their financial performance" (pfc social impact advisors 2019). To achieve this, it set out to create "the gold standard" for what every company must do in order to break even financially, economically, socially, and environmentally. It shows what a sustainable company looks like, and whether or not it is meeting a level of performance that takes society where it needs to go based on environmental and social science.

These levels of performance are expressed in the Future-Fit Business Benchmark, the core concept that underpins a suite of open-source materials that the Foundation provides to help companies assess their own level of fitness, and communicate their progress to stakeholders. The Benchmark articulates a set of goals that are reasonably generic across most businesses (i.e., not industry-specific). They are intended to be measurable in a reasonably simple way so that people can score progress from zero to 100% for every single goal. The Benchmark expands on the Future-Fit's core principles. Every core property is associated with actions which define what a company *must do* and what it *might do*. Must-do actions are called *Break-Even Goals*: if they are not met, natural and social systems are at risk. Might-do actions are called *Positive Pursuits*: they correct damage done to systems in the past and help others meet their goals.

There are 23 Break-Even Goals divided between the eight aforementioned properties. There are also 24 Positive Pursuits. The eight properties and their related goals/pursuits can be found at https://futurefitbusiness.org/explore-the-benchmark/. As an example, let us look at one property, Energy. People depend on natural systems to provide energy. Some sources of energy such as hydrocarbon fuels have a negative effect on system sustainability, causing climate change and pollution. In a Future-Fit Society, therefore, energy has to be non-finite (i.e., renewable) and not breach planetary boundaries. Those are the core properties, and the related Break-Even Goal is "Energy is from renewable sources." When a company achieves that goal, then in terms of energy it can said to be Future-Fit. While it is pursuing break-even, the company can also go further into the area called Positive Pursuits. Positive Pursuits are categories of action rather than specific goals, but they nonetheless articulate what might be meaningful in transforming to a Future-Fit Society. In the case of energy, for example, a Positive Pursuit might be actions that help others become less dependent on nonrenewable energy, or ones that enable more people to have access to energy.

Waste provides another useful example. The Break-Even Goals of eliminating operational waste and repurposing products give companies a clear steer where to apply their energies if we are to achieve a world without waste (Table 6.1). The goals direct the companies toward thinking about driving out waste, and where waste persists ensuring that products can be reused, recycled, or repurposed. This needs to be done without causing others to damage the environment. For example, it might not be enough to put liquids into recyclable bottles if the company knows customers cannot access appropriate recycling facilities. Or it might not be Future-Fit if a company's product specifications mean suppliers will produce waste that cannot be repurposed (e.g., offcuts from shoes contaminated with glue).

The Benchmark and related tools are free to use and are all available from the Foundation's website. They are designed to give companies a clear explanation of what to do and why. They explain what every business has to do and then what they might choose to do beyond that.

Table 6.1 Break-Even Goals for waste

Waste	
End State: In a Future-Fit Society, waste does not exist	
Break-Even Goal 1: Operational waste is eliminated	
Rationale: Waste means all materials generated as by-products of production and other operational activities which the company manages to contain, and which require treatment, repurposing, or disposal This includes both hazardous and non-hazardous manufacturing materials, as well as non-production waste such as office paper, food, and retired equipment	Company actions: To be Future-Fit, a company must: (a) eliminate all avoidable waste generation; and (b) reuse, recycle, or otherwise repurpose any remaining waste
Break-Even Goal 2: Products can be repurposed	
Rationale: A company must do all it can to ensure that any physical goods it provides to others can be responsibly repurposed at the end of their useful lives. This includes revenue-generating products, any packaging or other materials distributed to customers, along with any materials used to deliver services	Company actions: To be Future-Fit, a company must: (a) ensure that whatever remains of the goods it supplies can be separated at the end of their useful life, to maximize their post-use recovery value; and, (b) ensure that its customers have ready access to recovery services capable of extracting such value

They enable a company to see how close they are to the 23 different goals which themselves have a clear basis in science. Chris Davis, international director of corporate responsibility and campaigns, explains why he is using the Benchmark at The Body Shop: "This is the best available science from the smartest people we know. It is credible. Any other benchmark is not as comprehensive and doesn't cover your whole business" (pfc social impact advisors 2019).

The Body Shop is one of the companies adopting the Benchmark as central to its approach to understanding and acting on Wicked Problems. Others include Novo Nordisk, Eileen Fisher, Maersk, and De Beers. These firms are not looking for the rewards and prizes often associated with corporate social responsibility and nonfinancial reporting generally. FFF's the Foundation's offering is more orientated toward risk. It helps companies understand the risk they present to the rest of society—a salutary message but one that can be important when it comes to protecting reputation or attracting and retaining staff. It also helps them de-risk by avoiding catastrophic events, and as importantly it helps make companies ready to take advantage of new opportunities associated with social and environmental shifts.

Future-Fit, Future-Finance, Future-Technology

One of the issues the Future-Fit Business Benchmark was designed to address was the lack of comparability between industries that was typical of ESG analysis, something we discussed in Chapter 3. As we also noted in Chapter 4, in financial reporting, any company can be compared with another because the data collected are industry-neutral. However, when it comes to ESG performance, the data are often industry-specific so that comparisons between, for example, a mining company and a bank are impossible. The Business Benchmark makes companies comparable regardless of size or sector.

One thing this permits is taking a closer look at whether Big Technology is on a clear path to stay within planetary boundaries and where possible regenerate natural systems. Is Apple, for example, not only moving in the direction of using only renewable energy, but is it also reaching Break-Even Goals relating to water, pollution, waste, and the other social and natural system conditions? In terms of system value—the only value that matters in a future-fit world—how is Apple doing compared to Amazon and Alibaba? Looked at from a different perspective, the Business Benchmark means Big Tech cannot pick and choose which aspects of ESG performance it wants to highlight; rather, it needs to show the system value it delivers in relation to the full set of planetary boundaries.

FFF's business model also owes a lot to parts of Big Tech. Much of its offering is available for free such as the Business Benchmark, guidance on how to use the Benchmark, and detailed guidance on the Break-Even Goals and Positive Pursuits. It is an example of the open-source approach common in the ICT sphere. Software companies have long given away their software, and then sought to capitalize on it through training and advice. The Future-Fit Foundation is no different in this regard. A free but robust way to demonstrate and check the health of companies in a world of Wicked Problems could prove very valuable to companies and their investors, and once the user base is installed, other revenue streams should emerge.

In terms of scaling up the use of the Business Benchmark, Big Finance has a particular role to play, not just as a user, but as a promoter of future-fit thinking to other parts of the business world. Investors' role is fundamental to the Foundation's theory of change. FFF's ambition is that investors use the Benchmark when analyzing and engaging with companies. On the one hand, the Benchmark is promoted to companies as a tool for self-assessment, enabling them to set ambitions aligned with planetary health, and to make better day-to-day decisions. But at the same time, it is also promoted to investors as an assurance tool that provides consistent, comparable, and forward-looking information about what companies are doing. Those investors then insist companies use the Benchmark in their disclosures.

The pressure for action in FFF's theory of change therefore comes from two directions. First, companies themselves look to the Benchmark as a robust and consistent way to avoid risk and make them alert to opportunities. It helps them get a better understanding of where disruption is likely, and where disruption offers the potential for innovation. For instance, De Beers may not need to mine for diamonds if its lab-grown diamonds investment takes off. The Impossible Food Company offers tasty burgers but without the environmental impact of cattle by making its burgers from plants. IT, AI, and bioscience innovations are making it easier to be Future-Fit.

The second direction is pressure from investors. If nonfinancial information about companies was comparable, verifiable, and sufficient, then the long-anticipated potential of the investment community to drive change might be realized more rapidly and comprehensively than has hitherto been the case. But that hasn't happened. There is a lot of information being gathered about ESG, but it isn't considered consistent or meaningful enough to be included as an essential component of the investment process. Despite the amount of information being collected by companies, it is not useful for investors and does not allow them to decide which companies are future-fit or flabby. The Benchmark offers a way of assessing how fit companies are in a verifiable, understandable manner. However, they can only begin to do meaningful comparisons once enough companies are using the Benchmark. This means that in order for investors to exercise leverage over companies, they not only need to use the Benchmark, but they need the Benchmark to get to scale so there is a sufficiently large universe of companies to compare.

Companies using the Business Benchmark welcome a more active investor role. Indeed, they believe they have an important role to play even before the Benchmark is widely used. For example, different voices carry different amounts of weight within firms. If the head of sustainability says something, the CEO might listen and give it some thought. But if the head of investor relations brings up the exact same issue, the CEO pays much more attention. The frustration, though, is the pace of change. Cora Olsen, Novo Nordisk's global lead on integrated reporting, sighs, "What frustrates me is that the investors are usually 10 years behind. There is all this excitement when stock exchanges launch new ESG disclosure guidelines or guidance on metrics, but it's what we've been doing for 15 years" (pfc social impact advisors 2019).

Is Future-Fit Anything New?

Cora Olsen's frustration with the slow pace of change among investors is hints at a wider tension about whether it is companies or investors that are the obstacle to change. It is fair to ask, aren't there already enough initiatives for business to engage with? What is unique about the Future-Fit Foundation's offering? After all, there are all sorts of corporate responsibility endeavors, and there are reporting frameworks such as the Global Reporting Initiative and Integrated Reporting. Furthermore, the United Nations has created a blueprint for a sustainable future set out in its 17 Sustainable Development Goals. Is there a risk that FFF will add confusion rather than clarity?

One response to this is to point out that companies using existing standards and frameworks are only reporting on what they have done in the past, and this does nothing to explain to themselves or others the journey they are on. There is also a focus on best practice by sector, encouraged by sustainability rating systems such as FTSE4Good or DJSI. This tells us where companies are in relation to their peers, but not how they are benefiting society: it shows which companies are "least bad", but doesn't allow us to assess which ones are helping regeneration. Most of what exists today does not allow anyone to assess company progress toward and beyond the extra-financial break-even point.

A second response is that the Future-Fit Business Benchmark does not compete with, but rather complements, other nonfinancial reporting initiatives. Each Break-Even Goal can be mapped against the Sustainable Development Goals, and this is possible with one click on the Foundation's website. Likewise, the Benchmark may complement GRI and the Integrated Reporting framework. A comment heard from the Benchmark's supporters is that Future-Fit could be the Intel inside things like GRI or Integrated Reporting. It doesn't have to be visible, nor does it have to be the brand on the report, but it is what enables the report to have credibility and consistency.

The Future-Fit Theory of Change

FFF rejects the term nonfinancial reporting, preferring extra-financial to emphasize that social and environmental issues affect the company's financial health. The minute you call it nonfinancial, the CFO switches off. Its founders want to distance themselves from nonfinancial reporting's failure to get companies to take meaningful action in key areas of sustainability. In order to significantly expand the use and usefulness of extra-financial reporting among investors and companies, FFF has built its strategy around a theory of change. This is summarized in Fig. 6.3.

The overarching goal, as noted earlier, is to create a Future-Fit Society in which people as a whole live within planetary boundaries and enjoy the social foundations for humans to flourish. The goal of a Future-Fit Society informs all of the Foundation's work including the theory of change which comprises the following:

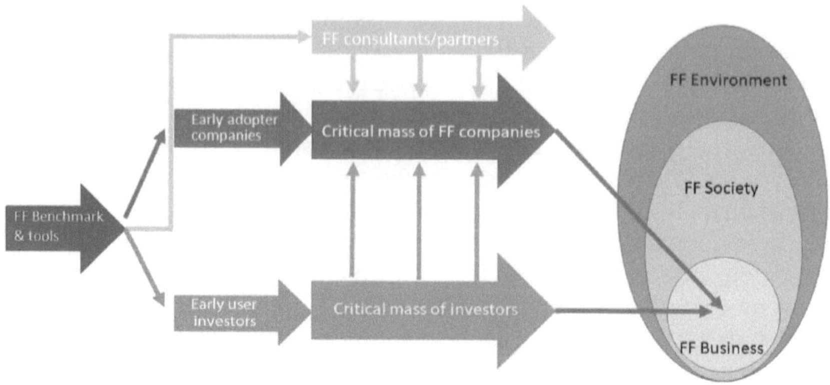

Fig. 6.3 Future-Fit Foundation's theory of change

- A science-based benchmark to help companies pursue the vision of a Future-Fit Society is made available for free.
- The Benchmark is promoted to companies as a tool for self-assessment, enabling them to set ambitions aligned with planetary health, and to make better day-to-day decisions.
- The Benchmark is also promoted to investors as an assurance tool that provides consistent, comparable, and forward-looking information about what companies are doing.
- Major companies become early adopters of the Benchmark, and generate interest from and further adoption by others.
- Accredited consultants assist companies to understand and use the Benchmark.
- Investors insist companies use the Benchmark in their disclosures.
- A global community of companies and investors uses the Benchmark to make management and investment decisions based on system value.

There are four assumptions about nonfinancial reporting behind this theory of change (Table 6.2).

These assumptions seem valid. There is considerable evidence that corporates already conducting ESG reporting find it burdensome and

Table 6.2 Assumptions underlying the Future-Fit offering

Assumption about present situation	*FFF response*
1. Corporates that already report on ESG matters find it burdensome, and don't find it useful for business decision-making	Develop a single science-based benchmark applicable to all companies and which facilities embedding sustainability into the core business
2. Corporates want to use nonfinancial reporting to guide business decision-making	Develop Break-Even Goals, Positive Pursuits, and accompanying guidance that are used to analyze and make decisions about sustainability investments and core business actions
3. Investors want to use nonfinancial reporting to make investment decisions	Promote the Future-Fit Business Benchmark to investors as a tool for exerting leverage over companies
4. Investors don't normally use nonfinancial reporting to make investment decisions because they don't see it as relevant to management processes or decision-making	Engage with companies and investors to examine why and how nonfinancial issues are material to business

unhelpful for decision-making (Assumption 1).[1] They want to use nonfinancial information to guide decision-making, and are already doing this to an extent (Assumption 2), although some feel they are reporting because it is a requirement others have imposed on them and forces them to look backward rather than think about future risks. Some investors, too, are using nonfinancial reporting (Assumption 3), but are struggling because the information is hard to verify, not comparable and is difficult to understand. This is one of the reasons nonfinancial reports are not made more use of, but it is also the case that a large number of investors do not think ESG issues are material (Assumption 4).

The fact these assumptions are valid strengthens the Foundation's case that its initiatives add value to, rather than replicate, what others are doing. FFF's collaboration with SASB (the Sustainability Accounting Standards Board), and the cross-referencing of the Business Benchmark with the SDGs are examples of what might evolve.

[1] See for instance the literature cited in pfc social impact advisors (2019).

Progress to Date

A lot of people now have heard about Future-Fit. Some of them still think we're a gym, but at least they've heard of us. Martin Rich

The profile of the Future-Fit Foundation seems to be on the rise. It may not have the name recognition of organizations and initiatives such as the Sustainable Development Goals, GRI or the Principles for Responsible Investment, but the Benchmark is getting used, the community is being built, and awareness is growing. The fact that progress cannot always be measured with hard numbers may not be a bad thing at this stage. The Foundation's model predicts that change will come about through a process. By working with a few large, well-known companies, it will have living examples of the Benchmark in use. These companies will reel in other companies, initially perhaps ones recognized as sustainability champions, but also including those who are worried about how to adapt to emergent challenges and Wicked Problems. This latter group accounts for the majority of large companies according to our interviewees, and once they see the advantages of becoming Future-Fit, the numbers become significant. The Foundation predicts that in ten years' time, there will be thousands of companies using the Benchmark, served by thousands of accredited consultants. Once this happens, laggard companies will be forced by investors, the public or their own survival to join the community of the Future-Fit.

In terms of measuring progress to date, what matters is whether the conditions of change are in place. Are well-known companies active on the Foundation's Development Council that initiates change? Yes. Are investors involved as well? Yes, although not yet the cross-section of the investment community that the Foundation would like. Are consultants being accredited? Yes. Is the Benchmark getting recognition? Yes, although as we have seen in the section on nonfinancial reporting, it is in a crowded space where there is confusion, overlap, and perhaps frustration about the plethora of initiatives.

Beyond this, there is anecdotal evidence of impact. Cora Olsen of Novo Nordisk says she has seen Future-Fit get a lot of interest from companies already interested in sustainability or corporate social responsibility, but for her what validates the investment her company has made to date are the requests for meetings from small- and medium-sized companies or ones that do not have a sustainability profile. Smaller consultancies with accredited Future-Fit consultants such as Proxima and Nordic Sustainability are using the Benchmark with certain clients.

However, as with any kind of impact, it is not always easy to attribute causation. For example, a company might have been engaging with Future-Fit at a certain level of management but without huge progress in terms of company-wide change. Then there is a change of ownership, spurring transformation across the business. Suddenly, the company's owners commit to delivering on a triple bottom line. This is what has happened at The Body Shop when it was bought by Natura. The company's long-standing involvement in Future-Fit was opportune as the new management began to rethink value, but it is the change in ownership rather than the Future-Fit concept that has enabled the company to become more ambitious in its sustainability activities.

Equally, the open-source nature of the Benchmark means that it may not always be used in the way it was intended. Alicia Ayars at the Foundation has seen the Future-Fit materials used in a way that is not aligned with the spirit with which they were intended. "While we have Accredited Partners, we're very aware that there are other consultants who are using the Future-Fit Business Benchmark. We're happy for them to do that. The problem comes when they've gone through the process of measuring a company's progress indicators, but they've taken out the bits that the company doesn't like. That happens" (as cited in pfc social impact advisors 2019 p. 13).

Companies around the world face Wicked Problems resulting from growing populations, planetary boundaries pushed to breaking point, weak social foundations, and increasingly wealthy consumers. In a Future-Fit Society, business will make a positive contribution to a regenerative, flourishing natural environment, and the creation of strong social foundations that will enable all people to thrive. The Future-Fit Foundation is helping build community where stakeholders can contribute and learn from each other in ways imagined in Deliberate Leadership. In fact, many qualities of Deliberate Leadership are reflected in FFF's approach. Courage, candor, and creativity are features of Deliberate Leadership and of the Foundations. Not that change will happen overnight. One of the 7Cs of Deliberate Leadership is "compassion," realigning the power dynamics surrounding an organization so that it is more empathetic of others. The shift toward "system value" that the Business Benchmark calls for requires companies to consider their impact on suppliers, and reconsider the tense, competitive relationships that have been typical between suppliers and buyers in the past. However, this type of change will take time, and as the impact of Wicked Problems increases, will Deliberate Leadership result in rates of transition that are unacceptably slow? As environmentalist and FFF supporter, Bob Willard, points out, the strengths of the Benchmark could be its weakness. "The Benchmark's extremely rigorous, very comprehensive, wonderfully thought out. The bad news is it's very rigorous, very comprehensive, wonderfully thought out. It's complicated. It looks complicated. And that's the challenge that the Benchmark has" (as cited in pfc social impact advisors 2019, p. 10).

Conclusion

Time and again throughout this book we have portrayed a world in which the activities and influence of Big Finance and Big Technology are so strong that they not only intrude into every aspect of our lives, they come to define what is normal. We have also shown a world that is full of Wicked Problems: ones that cannot be solved in ways that linear problems once could, but which nonetheless need tackling if life on earth is to prosper. Our old ways of thinking evident for instance in classical economics and financing accounting, add to rather than remedy those problems. But in their place new ways of thinking and behaving are emerging including the new economic ideas of Raworth, Perez, and Mazzucato (Chapter 1), and new ways of understanding organizations' value and performance such as impact accounting and social finance (Chapter 4).

However, the gap between Big Finance and Big Technology and the potential for having positive social impact is more like a gorge than a crevice. The needs of vulnerable people and our planet, as set out for instance in the SDGs, require the engagement of Big Finance and Big Technology. They are two of the most prominent actors with the power and influence to address the Wicked Problems affecting natural and social systems. But without a common understanding about what kinds of social and environmental impact are positive, and a redistribution of power and voice, the gap will remain even as Finance and Technology claim to be contributing to reaching the SDGs. Until this situation is addressed, the world of "Big" risks locking people in a degenerative system rather than the regenerative one required for share prosperity.

This book provides an overview of the issues and approaches social investors should consider to avoid harm and maximize positive contributions when tackling the world's most challenging problems. It shares successes and cautionary tales from seasoned academics, advocates, and advisors based on extensive research which included 1500 interviews with social finance leaders in 20 countries. It is designed to help investors in philanthropy, impact investing, and traditional finance find their North Star as leaders in the field. It reveals the range of initiatives needed to enable purposeful change, ranging from setting benchmarks, building the capacity to manage transformation processes, and experimenting with different forms of social finance, to creating communities of experts and practitioners, product innovation, and measuring impact. The old economy's financial accounting is able to maintain its dominant position because it has a well-developed ecosystem comprising multiple complementary actors. In order to achieve the vision of sustainability set out in the SDGs, a similar ecosystem is required to support impact investing, social finance, and impact accounting. Partners for a New Economy is one of the organizations that is providing support for a transformation ecosystem that includes developing new economic theory, fostering initiatives to enable new types of value to become the norm, and helping to scale up innovation through education and business engagement.

Throughout this book, we have provided examples and opinions about what is being done and why. In Chapter 6, in particular, we have provided two detailed case studies, each showing in different ways how Big Finance can consciously, demonstrably, and responsibly bring about social and environmental change. The lessons we have identified are based on the principles of Deliberate Leadership, grounded in core values shared by most successful social investors: courage to recognize the complexity of the circumstances; collaboration by embracing diverse perspectives; community feedback and partnership must guide investment; creativity is essential in imagining and testing different scenarios; candor to speak the truth and recalibrate investment based on facts; capital is defined by social, environmental, and financial assets; and compassion to walk with empathy and in the shoes of those you seek to help.

These are the toughest of times, and challenges are emerging thick and fast. What with climate change, racism, threats to democracy, a health pandemic, and international border tensions all coming together at the same time, Wicked Problems have become the drumbeat of modern life.

It is encouraging to see that the challenges are being addressed in innovative ways. However, looking at the dark side and the perils associated with Big Finance and Big Technology, it is clear just how much effort will be required to put us on the kind of course organizations such as the Future-Fit Foundation and Social Value International, or individuals such as Tom van Dyck want to see. But as *Guardian* journalist, Richard Flanagan, reminds us our hope is tied to our courage and the values that ground us in our aspirations and our actions for impact.

References

Barker, R., and Robert Eccles. 2018. *Should FASB and IASB be responsible for setting standards for nonfinancial information?*. Oxford: Said Business School.

Brookings Institution. (2018). *Educate Girls Development Impact Bond: Year 3 Results*. Washington, DC: Brookings Institution.

Bukhari, A., & Husain, S. (2016). *Triggering Success: Innovative Interventions to Promote Educational Access in India*. Educate Girls, UBS Optimus Foundation. https://www.educategirls.ngo/pdf/Triggering%20Success%20Innovative%20Interventions%20to%20Promote%20Educational%20Access.pdf.

pfc social impact advisors. 2018. *UBS Optimus Foundation: From Giving to Investing*. (G. Peterson, Ed.). St. Paul, MN: Oxford Impact Investing and Social Finance Programmes.

pfc social impact advisors. 2019. *Future-Fit Foundation: A New Benchmarking Paradigm for Business in Achieving the UN Sustainable Development Goals*.

UBS Optimus Foundation. (2017). *Impact First: Annual Review 2016 of UBS Optimus Foundation Network*. Zürich, Switzerland: UBS.

Correction to: Promise and Peril of Big Finance

Correction to:
Chapter 3 in: G. Peterson et al., *Navigating Big Finance and Big Technology for Global Change*, Palgrave Studies in Impact Finance, https://doi.org/10.1007/978-3-030-40712-4_3

The original version of this chapter has been revised with some belated corrections. The chapter has been updated with the changes.

The updated version of this chapter can be found at
https://doi.org/10.1007/978-3-030-40712-4_3

G. Peterson et al., *Navigating Big Finance and Big Technology for Global Change*, Palgrave Studies in Impact Finance,
https://doi.org/10.1007/978-3-030-40712-4_7

Index

G. Peterson et al., *Navigating Big Finance and Big Technology for Global Change*, Palgrave Studies in Impact Finance,
https://doi.org/10.1007/978-3-030-40712-4

GPSR Compliance
The European Union's (EU) General Product Safety Regulation (GPSR) is a set of rules that requires consumer products to be safe and our obligations to ensure this.

If you have any concerns about our products, you can contact us on

ProductSafety@springernature.com

In case Publisher is established outside the EU, the EU authorized representative is:

Springer Nature Customer Service Center GmbH
Europaplatz 3
69115 Heidelberg, Germany

www.ingramcontent.com/pod-product-compliance
Ingram Content Group UK Ltd.
Pitfield, Milton Keynes, MK11 3LW, UK
UKHW040225290926
15471UKWH00001B/5
* 9 7 8 3 0 3 0 4 0 7 1 4 8 *